THE PRICE OF EVERYTHING

THE PRICE OF EVERYTHING

A Parable of Possibility and Prosperity

Russell Roberts

PRINCETON UNIVERSITY PRESS

PRINCETON & OXFORD

Grateful acknowledgment is made for permission to reprint an excerpt
from the film *K-Pax*, copyright © 2001 Universal Studios and
Intermedia Film.

Pages 171–172: "The Summer Day" from *House of Light* by
Mary Oliver, copyright © 1990 by Mary Oliver, reprinted by
permission of Beacon Press, Boston.

Published by Princeton University Press, 41 William Street, Princeton,
New Jersey 08540

In the United Kingdom: Princeton University Press, 6 Oxford Street,
Woodstock, Oxfordshire OX20 1TW

Seventh printing, and first paperback printing, 2009

Library of Congress Control Number: 2008927632

ISBN: 978-0-691-14335-4 (pbk.)

ISBN: 978-0-691-13509-0 (cloth)

British Library Cataloging-in-Publication Data is available

This book has been composed in Bembo and Engravers

Printed on acid-free paper ∞

press.princeton.edu

Printed in the United States of America

14 15 16 17 18 19 20

To Sharon, my weaver of dreams

An economist knows the price of everything and the value of nothing.
— Anonymous paraphrase
of Oscar Wilde's definition of a cynic

The basic mystery about ant colonies is that there is no management. A functioning organization with no one in charge is so unlike the way humans operate as to be virtually inconceivable. There is no central control. No insect issues commands to another or instructs it to do things in a certain way. No individual is aware of what must be done to complete any colony task. Each ant scratches and prods its way through the tiny world of its immediate surroundings. Ants meet each other, separate, go about their business. Somehow, these small events create a pattern that drives the coordinated behavior of colonies.
— Deborah Gordon, *Ants at Work*

You know what I've learned about your planet? There's enough life on earth to fill fifty planets. Plants, animals, people, fungi, viruses. All jostling to find their place. Bouncing off each other. Feeding off each other. Connected.
— Spoken by the character Prot
in the movie *K-Pax*

The curious task of economics is to demonstrate to men how little they really know about what they imagine they can design.
— F. A. Hayek, *The Fatal Conceit*

Contents

Author's Note

This book is set in the near future. Ramon Fernandez, Ruth Lieber, and the people they encounter in this story are products of my imagination. Any resemblance to real people on the Stanford Campus is purely coincidental. There is no Big Box corporation—any resemblance of its CEO, Bob Bachman, to a real person is purely coincidental. The other companies and people and events mentioned in this book are real or at least as real as can be imagined as this book goes to press. I have tried to portray them along with the facts about America and the American economy as accurately as possible. Sources and additional readings can be found at the back of the book.

THE PRICE OF EVERYTHING

1

THINKING OUTSIDE THE BOX

Just past midnight on a July night in Havana, the woman wakes and hears the tap, tap, tap at the window. She opens the door and the man, her brother, comes in and scoops up the sleeping boy, carrying him on his shoulder like a bundle of sugarcane. They head out into the sweltering streets. The woman carries a string bag and a blanket. Can a string bag contain a life? It must. It's all she can take with her. The boy sleeps on as they walk into the night.

Getting to the outskirts of the city and to the beach beyond seems to take an eternity. They wade out to the small boat waiting for them in the shallows and climb aboard.

The boy opens his eyes. The woman hugs him back to sleep. When she thinks back on that night, she remembers clutching her son, prayer after prayer, and the boat, endlessly rocking, heading north.

"Sold out."

Sold out? Home Depot sold out of flashlights? It was impossible. How could they be sold out?

"What do you mean?" Ramon Fernandez asked.

"Sorry," the clerk replied. "This place has been a madhouse for the last two hours. I wish I could tell you there are more in the back. But there aren't. They're gone. Every one of them. Come back in a few days."

Earlier that evening, Ramon and Amy had been making dinner when the floor began to shake. The earthquake seemed to go on and on, the glasses and plates rattling and tinkling on the kitchen shelves and two pictures crashing off the wall. Then the lights went out. Ramon lit the candles he had already set out for dinner and they enjoyed the meal rather than rushing out. Evidently a few hundred people had beat them to Home Depot in search of flashlights.

"Hey, wait a minute," the clerk said. "Aren't you Ramon Fernandez?"

Ramon just smiled and moved on. He was used to people recognizing him. The best tennis player at Stanford since John McEnroe, he had won the NCAA singles title for the last three years and had made it to the finals of Wimbledon last year. He was probably the best-known twenty-year-old in the Bay Area. Maybe the best-known twenty-year-old in the country. Even people who didn't care about tennis or sports knew the story of how his mother had fled Cuba in a small boat and somehow made it to Florida when Ramon was a kid.

"Do you think we'll have better luck finding milk or ice for the cooler?" Amy asked once they were back in the car. "Or should we just give up?"

"How about Big Box in Hayward?"

"Big Box?"

"That new chain—combination Home Depot, Sam's Club, and Border's. They say the back of the store's in a different time zone than the front. Or at least another zip code. It's probably our best chance to get milk and maybe they'll have a flashlight. Or a lantern. Or a laser. Or something. They're supposed to sell everything."

"Alright. I've got a full tank of gas. Let's give it a shot."

Big Box's beginnings in the Bay Area had been rocky. A referendum kept them out of San Francisco. Berkeley residents marched against the store that had tried to open there. So far, the only store that had made it was in Hayward, just south of Oakland.

Amy and Ramon fought their way across the San Mateo Bridge to the 880 and up to Hayward. Big Box made a Home Depot store look like a 7-11. The Big Box parking lot was so large that shuttle buses took shoppers from their cars to the front door. Once inside, most customers rode mini-shuttles, custom-designed oversized golf carts that took you to the different regions of the store on mechanized routes, like little trams or trolleys. Some families took their kids just to ride the mini-shuttles and try the free samples scattered throughout the store. Or parents could drop off their kids in the giant Legoland in the center of the store while they shopped.

Ramon and Amy arrived just after midnight. The parking lot was crowded but they had no trouble finding a place and boarding a shuttle. Getting into the store proved to be the problem. An angry mob surged around the main door, yelling and chanting. Amy and Ramon couldn't figure out what was going on. They pushed forward and then they saw it. A large sign had been posted just inside the entrance: TONIGHT ONLY, ALL PRICES, DOUBLE THE MARKED PRICE. An anti-sale! And from the looks of it, a public relations disaster was also in progress.

An employee with a megaphone stood on a pile of bags of mulch, trying to calm the crowd. The decision had come out of Omaha, he explained—there was nothing he could do about it. In his hand was a set of postcards, comment forms that he was eager to give out to defuse the crowd and preserve his health. The group milling around the front door didn't seem very interested in the postcards. They were looking for a more visceral and immediate form of feedback and customer satisfaction.

Beyond the mob at the door, the store looked like it always did. The trams were busy and crowded with people shopping despite the surcharge. "Unbelievable," Ramon muttered under his breath. "Want to leave?" he asked Amy.

"I want a flashlight. And I wouldn't mind getting some milk if they have it. We're here. I know it's a rip-off, but I'm scared. I don't have any candles. We don't know how long it'll be before things get back to normal."

They stayed. They had no trouble finding the milk and the flashlights. They also picked up some extra batteries just in case. Only three checkout lanes were open, but Amy and Ramon didn't mind waiting a little longer than usual.

They always found plenty to talk about. They had met freshman year at a meeting for athletes on scholarship to help them negotiate the labyrinth of NCAA rules and regulations. Ramon asked to borrow a pen from the tall blonde volleyball player sitting next to him. They started talking and found they had almost nothing in common. She was the daughter of a U.S. senator. She had grown up in Georgetown and had attended an exclusive private school. She was majoring in biology and planned to go to med school. Ramon grew up in poverty in Miami. His mother was a cleaning woman. He was studying political science. She was blonde and he was dark. She played volleyball. He played tennis. At least both of their sports had nets, he joked. They kept talking, despite their differences. He asked her to a movie that night and soon they were spending a lot of time together, whatever time they could spare between working out, practices, class time, and homework.

Standing in line at Big Box, Amy and Ramon's conversation was interrupted by a wild cacophony of noise coming from the front of the line. A woman was screaming in Spanish. In one hand she held a jar of baby food. With her other hand she held a baby on her hip. Both items looked dangerous to the cashier, who had her hands up in defense and whose entreaties in English were getting nowhere. Then, the woman stopped yelling and burst into tears. The baby, cued by the mother's crying, began to wail. The checker stood there mutely, trying to figure out what to do.

Ramon came to the front of the line, put his hand on the woman's shoulder and spoke softly to her in Spanish. The woman stopped crying. Then the baby stopped crying. The checker smiled, hoping that the impasse was over.

Ramon explained to the people waiting in line that the woman had $20 but the bill was $35. How could she have known that Big Box would gouge her with doubled prices? When the cashier had suggested that she do without some of the items, the woman had gone berserk. How could she not bring home food and diapers for her children?

Ramon took off his Stanford baseball cap, put $2 in and asked if anyone else in the line could help out. In under a minute, the other people in the line had come up with the $15 to close the gap. At first the woman refused to accept the money. But Ramon kept talking quietly to her and finally, she took the money and finished checking out. Ramon told Amy to check out without him. He stayed with the Mexican woman, talking all the while.

When Amy got outside, she found Ramon up on the stacked bags of mulch in front of the store. Next to him was the Mexican woman with her baby. Next to her was the same Big Box employee they'd seen before at the front of the store. He looked as if he wanted to run away. But Ramon was using the megaphone that belonged to Big Box. The employee felt he ought to stay close to company property. The crowd had grown a lot larger and a lot quieter. Seeing Ramon Fernandez up on a mulch mountain with a megaphone at one in the morning made people stop to see what was going on.

"What kind of store decides to profit off of hungry children and a caring mother? We need to send a message to Omaha!" The crowd roared back its approval. Amy marveled at Ramon's initiative and style. He looked as relaxed and natural as he did on a tennis court. Ramon went on for a while and got the crowd good and angry. If he had given the word, they'd have smashed every window at the front of the store. But he had a different plan. Instead, he lowered his voice and slowed his cadence. He spoke about the desperation of poverty and the need to restrain corporate power. The people in the crowd looked up at him, transfixed. When he was done, they applauded and started filling out the complaint cards.

2

OUT OF CONTROL

Some say Ramon's father was the greatest baseball player ever to come out of Cuba. Some say he was the greatest baseball player, ever, period, full stop, no qualifiers. In the stories the mother tells, Jose Fernandez always wins the game with a home run or a diving catch or a throw to the plate from center field on a line that was as straight as a dart or an arrow or a gunshot or a frozen rope. The crowd chants his name over and over until he emerges from the dugout and tips his hat. All of the stories she tells are true. Her father was an accountant for the national team and as a girl of fifteen, she saw her future husband for the first time when he went four for five and went to the wall with perfect timing and turned a home run into an out. He was twenty-one and already a man among boys.

In his prime, even past his prime, men approach Jose Fernandez with promises of riches waiting for him in America if only he will come to the Yankees or the Reds or the Dodgers. They tell him of his teammates who have left and how they live—the good American life with a big house and a fancy car and anything else the heart or head desires. But he stays. Cuba's fortunes rise and fall, but still he stays. He retires holding every significant batting record in Cuban baseball. Castro makes him an ambassador for the game on the streets of the capital and in the small towns. Only Castro can draw a larger crowd on a stroll through the streets.

When Ramon is born, there are celebrations throughout the island. Even the Great Leader sends flowers and best wishes for

the boy's future. When the baby comes home from the hospital,
Castro comes to the house. There is a picture in the paper of Castro
holding the infant, beaming.

In Ruth Lieber's office, bookshelves went floor to ceiling
and on some of the shelves, the books were lined up two deep,
with more books wedged sideways into the gaps above the
books. In the middle of the room, ziggurats of books soared
up from a large library table.

Every decade or so, to the amusement and teasing of her
colleagues, Ruth cleared off her desk and the table in the
center of the office. One September, years ago, shortly after
she had done a summer cleaning and the office was fairly tidy,
Ruth found a student sitting at the table reading, sipping a
cup of coffee. She recognized him as one of the new graduate
students. She sat down behind the desk and waited for him to
introduce himself, to tell her why he was there. But minutes
passed in silence, Ruth waiting, the student reading. Finally
Ruth asked if she could help him. It turned out that he had
thought her office was the departmental library. He thought
he'd sit and read for a while, do a little work.

It became a famous story in the department, but the story
was more than a tribute to the number of books Ruth owned
and the peculiar habits of first-year graduate students. In a real
sense, Ruth's office was the department's library and Ruth
was the librarian. Ruth had actually read most of the books
and even remembered most of what was in them. So in the
pre-Internet age, asking Ruth to find a quote or a fact was
the closest you could get to Google.

This was one of those years when the table was covered
with books, the desk was covered with books, there were

even books piled on the floor, a cityscape of books, a skyline towering everywhere. Ruth sat at the desk, embraced by her library, preparing for her first lecture of the spring quarter. Her mind kept wandering as she thought about how strange it was to be teaching her last economics course.

She had been at the university for over forty years. Most of the time, she had been a professor of economics, doing research in American economic history. In the middle of her career, she had made a conscious decision to be more of a teacher than a scholar. In many economics departments, there is one exceptional teacher who teaches the large introductory classes to hundreds of students each year. Ruth was that teacher.

Late in her career, she had become provost. She really had no time for teaching, but she insisted on doing it anyway, one class a year, a senior seminar limited to twenty students. She planned to retire in the fall, so this was her last class.

Entering the classroom, she took the seat nearest the blackboard at the head of the massive oak table that took up most of the room, and introduced herself. Then she took a pencil, a newly sharpened Dixon Ticonderoga #2, out of her briefcase and put it down on the table in front of her.

"No one can make a pencil."

Ruth let the statement sit there. She looked at the students' faces. They weren't quite sure how to react. Was she challenging them? Kidding them?

A student raised his hand.

"Your name?" Ruth asked.

"Josh."

"What do you think, Josh? True or false? Agree or disagree? No one can make a pencil."

"Seems silly," he said, taking a chance, then added, "with all due respect. You can buy pencils at the campus bookstore and all over town. People leave them lying around. They're practically everywhere."

"Can you make one, Josh?"

"What? A pencil? Of course not."

"Why of course not?"

"I'm twenty-one years old, I'm—"

"Do you think I could make one?"

Josh took it as a rhetorical question. Two down, another 6 billion or so to go, he thought to himself. "We'd probably have better luck visiting a pencil factory and looking for some better candidates," he said.

"Actually, I have visited a pencil factory," Ruth said. "No one there knows how to make a pencil, either. What do you think you'd find in a pencil factory?"

"A bunch of people making pencils." The class laughed and everyone relaxed a little bit. "A bunch of pencil-making equipment," Josh continued. "Some wood. Some lead. Some erasers. The people put them together. How hard could it be?"

"Ever wonder how they get the lead in there?" Ruth asked.

"I don't know," Josh said. He'd never thought about it. But he took a stab anyway. "They probably take a piece of wood, shape it like a pencil and drill a hole, drop in the lead. No?"

Ruth was shaking her head. She reached down into her briefcase again and pulled out what appeared to be a thin piece of wood.

"There's only one place in the world that makes these cedar slats and sells them to pencil factories. In the factory, they put ten narrow grooves, each the width of a pencil lead, into each slat, like this."

She reached down into her bag and pulled out a second cedar slat with ten grooves cut into it.

"Then they put a little glue in the grooves and lay a lead in each groove. Of course it's not really lead, it's graphite. Anybody know where graphite comes from?"

Nobody answered, so Ruth continued.

"It's found underground in Sri Lanka, in Mexico, in China, in Brazil. At the pencil factory, they mix it with clay from Mississippi and a little water and bake it, if that's the right word for cooking something at 1900 degrees. Then they roll it out and cut it so it's the right length. Voila! What we call pencil lead. They put the lead in these grooves and then they take another grooved cedar slat and lay it on top. A lead and cedar sandwich. It looks like this."

She reached down again into the briefcase and pulled out another piece of wood.

"What I really wanted to bring back from the factory," Ruth continued, "was the pencil in the lobby. Maybe 30 feet long. A perfect super-jumbo replica of a real pencil, down to the eraser. Just in case Paul Bunyan or King Kong stopped by and needed something to write with. Now look at this cedar sandwich. There are ten pencils imprisoned in here. We need to set them free. So they pass this sandwich through a special saw that carves the pencils from this block. First they cut off the bottom so it looks like this. Can you see the pencils peeking out? These are going to be classic six-sided pencils. Here you can see them half-cut. Then they turn the slat upside down, pass it through the saw again, and ten pencils emerge. Then each one gets painted three times, that beautiful canary yellow. Ever notice how there's never any paint smeared on the end you sharpen? How do they paint it so perfectly?"

"They use special tiny brushes?" Josh guessed.

"That's right. A gnome casts a magic spell on some elves. The elves, entranced, use the brushes to get it just right. Actually, they make the pencil a little too long. After they paint it, they slice a titch off the end so that it looks clean. I love that! Isn't that marvelous? Better than elves! But they don't worry if the other end is a little sloppy because the customer never sees that end—it's covered up by the little piece of aluminum and the eraser. After the aluminum and the eraser, they stamp the green letters on. That neon green you see in the body of a fly if the light's right. But you know what my favorite part of the whole process is? The cedar shavings. When they carve out the pencils from the cedar sandwich with the three-sided saw, one side at a time, little bits of cedar are left behind. The EPA won't let them just throw them out. So, you know what they do?"

"Build little cedar houses for the elves?" Josh joked.

"You're getting into it, aren't you, Josh? But no, instead of having to dispose of them the way the EPA demands, they get turkey farmers to come and pick up the shavings—they use them for bedding for the turkeys. Turkeys like sitting on those shavings, so the farmers are willing to come get them. The pencil company has to get rid of them, so they save money on disposal. There's something poignant to me about those comfortable turkeys sitting on that luxurious cedar bedding in October, totally oblivious to what happens toward the end of November."

Ruth paused and looked around the room.

"A simple pencil," she said, holding up the pencil and turning it this way and that in the winter light streaming in from the giant windows lining the wall. "Is there anything

simpler? Yet the making of a pencil is almost—" She paused
to find the right word. "Magical. Is it absurd to call something so simple and mundane, magical? But it's an achieve-
ment on the order of a jazz quartet improvising a tune when
the band members are in separate cities. Something that on
the surface seems impossible, but somehow, comes together.
What's your name?" Ruth asked, pointing to a girl sitting in
the back who looked distinctly unimpressed.

"Andrea."

"What do you think, Andrea. Magical or not magical?"

"It's nice, Professor Lieber. But it's just a pencil, isn't it?"

"Are you sure? Is that your final answer? Just a pencil?
Start with the plain, simple slat. A cedar tree in California
has to be chopped down, then taken to a mill. They fashion
that tree into a slat. That seemingly simple act of chopping
down the tree, getting it to the mill, and planing and shaping the wood—that takes thousands of people who work
in the woods, who build the saws that work the trees, who
drive the trucks that carry the timber, who make the trucks
that the trucker drives, who work in the mill that shapes
the logs, who make the machinery in the mill. And that's
just the wood. Then there's the graphite that goes into the
lead. Countless people in Sri Lanka, say, are at work, carving
it out of the ground and getting it to the factory. The aluminum ferrule is from Japan. The eraser is synthetic rubber
from Korea or sometimes Canada. And the lacquer that gives
it that nice sunshine shine—that's from Tennessee or New
Jersey. Those are just the basic components. And when it gets
to the factory, there are all the people who work putting the
pieces together. They use machines designed and created by
another huge group of people. No one person could do all

that. It would take thousands of lifetimes. No one can make a pencil."

"So a lot of people work on a pencil," Andrea said. "People specialize. What's the big deal? Where's the magic?"

"Who commands the army?"

"What?"

"Who commands the army?"

"What army?"

"The army that worked to put this pencil together. Who's in charge? Where's the general of this army of effort? Where is the pencil czar? Who is it?"

"Why would you need one?" Andrea asked.

"Every year, the right amount of cedar is cut to make all the pencils, the right amount of graphite gets pulled out of the ground, even though both of those products are used for a thousand other things. Why is there always enough to go around? The waitress never says to the truck driver, 'Sorry, hon,—we're out of coffee today.' The mill never runs out of cedar. And when you show up at the campus bookstore in September or even in January, there are always plenty of pencils to buy, whether you want one or a dozen. The bookstore never says, 'Sorry, we're out of pencils, but come back in July, our supplier expects to have some then.' And that's just the beginning. Who decides how many people are going to be in this army? Who decides what their jobs are? Who tells the people all over the world who work on the parts of the pencil what to do and when? Who makes sure that all the workers do their jobs well? Somehow, a million people spread out over the face of the earth work together. But no one coordinates that effort. The Sri Lankan graphite miner never communicates with the truck driver bringing the cedar into the pencil factory. That's why it's something akin to playing jazz with three other people spread out across the country. There's no script. No score. No conductor. Isn't that extraordinary?"

The class was quiet. They weren't sure how to respond. Rapture from a teacher in the classroom was unusual. Rapture about a pencil was off the charts.

"To notice it," Ruth continued, "to notice the magic of a pencil, it's not enough to pay attention. The magic is hidden. It's a sort of silent music, the music of the pencil. But you can hear it in your head, once you understand it. The source of the music, the source of the magic is what Adam Smith called 'the propensity to truck, barter, and exchange one thing for another.' Smith understood that order can emerge without someone being in charge to impose the order from above. Just from people buying and selling with each other. You can have a system that is organized without an organizer. What holds this system together? What creates the web of cooperation between all the different people who had a hand in getting this pencil into my hand? Yes, your name?"

"Amy. Can I ask a question about your question?"

"Sure."

"You say that no one's in charge. But that pencil factory you went to had a boss. The workers don't just show up, do their own thing and voila! A pencil emerges! There's someone ordering the wood, someone ordering the aluminum, ordering the rubber, hiring workers, supervising the workers, deciding what to pay them, sometimes firing workers. Someone decides whether to buy graphite or make it at the factory. It's not really spontaneous. Someone's in charge."

"It's an illusion."

"What do you mean?" Amy asked. "That people have a lot of autonomy in an organization?"

"Oh, that's true, too," Ruth responded. "But I meant something more complex. I meant it's an illusion that the boss is in charge. It looks like the boss gets to decide who to hire and who to fire, what to pay people and whether to have a cedar farm or buy cedar from another company. The boss doesn't even get to set the price of the pencil."

"But if it isn't the boss making those decisions, who makes them?" Amy asked.

"No one." Ruth stopped talking for a moment and let that sink in. The room suddenly seemed very quiet. I love teaching and I love economics, Ruth thought to herself. "Understanding how that can possibly be true is what we're going to spend the rest of the quarter trying to understand," she said. "In the meanwhile, homework!" She paced in front of the class. "For next class, think of something from the world around us that is self-organized. Find something that shows order or purpose even though no one's in charge of it. Look around. It's everywhere."

3

Birds of a Feather

Jose Fernandez is standing at home plate giving a batting exhibition in a distant province when he collapses. A hush falls over the small stadium. They rush him to the nearest hospital but it is too late. His death is a day of national mourning on the island. The people say he played too hard for too long and simply wore out his heart. His wife Celia hears rumors that the ambulance went to the wrong hospital where the right equipment was missing, but what is to be done?

Castro attends the funeral and the tears and speeches flow for days. When it is over, and after a week and then a month have passed, things are different. Slowly, the special treatment Celia had become accustomed to is taken away. She has to move from her house. She has to leave her job and the new one does not pay as well. She looks to the future and sees that if her son has even a fraction of his father's gifts, he will be useful to Castro. Ramon will be taken from her and put into a sports academy. He will get the best instruction. He will become a baseball player like his father whether he likes it or not. She will be rewarded. She will get her house back and her job and all that she had become accustomed to. The life she had will be rebuilt. Is that any use of a boy? Her brother Eduardo knows a man with a boat. They make a plan.

When the woman and the boy leave Cuba, Castro calls in the Minister of Sports and tells him to erase Jose Fernandez from all the record books. Take down all the plaques. Destroy the statue in the square of the town where he was born. Obliterate his memory forever.

Ramon met Heavy Weather and some of his friends for lunch that Sunday at a Thai place in Palo Alto off of University. Everybody in Berkeley knew Heavy Weather but no one knew whether he was closer to thirty or fifty. Some said that his parents had been radicals back in the 1960s, that they had been into some very heavy stuff with the Panthers and they had done jail time. Some said that Heavy Weather had made those stories up, that he was just a perpetual grad student in sociology with a wistful longing for the glory days of the past. What no one doubted was his fascination with the aesthetics of protest and street theater as a political art form. When rich bureaucrats met to discuss the World Trade Organization or trade policy or aid to the developing nations, Heavy was there. He had been in Seattle and Washington and Geneva and Doha. He had an innate skill for organization and some very large e-mail lists of like-minded people.

And while no one was really sure whether Heavy Weather was really his name or not, whether it was a moment of '60s inspiration from his parents or self-imposed, it was clear that at this stage of his life the first part of his name was ironic— he was more stick-like than stocky. He was six feet tall but couldn't have weighed more than 165 pounds. Along with his love for protest and street antics, he was obsessed with biking and fitness. He had the gaunt physique of the marathon runner. He didn't own a car, didn't know how to drive one, and had no driver's license. He thought nothing of biking from Berkeley to Palo Alto for lunch. Enjoyed it, actually.

Heavy Weather had heard about the Big Box price mark-ups the night of the earthquake. Someone had told him that Ramon Fernandez had been there, center stage, and Heavy wondered whether it might make some sense for the two of them to join forces. Heavy was always looking for an opportunity to strike a blow against corporate oppression—he immediately saw the value of exploiting Ramon's high profile.

They spent the first part of lunch debating where to hold the protest. Ramon wanted to hold it at the Big Box Executive Education Center—part of the Stanford Business School—a cedar and glass jewel nestled in the hills on the edge of campus. One of Heavy's confederates wanted it at Berkeley, where the locals and the large population of sympathetic students could be counted on to swell the crowd. The group argued the pros and cons of each location for over an hour.

Eventually, the tide turned toward Stanford. Big Box was a big enough target that it would be easy to convince students from Berkeley to make the trip across the Bay. The only worry was that the Stanford administration might shut the whole thing down or limit its effectiveness by cordoning off the protesters to a part of campus that would be less telegenic or less effective in mobilizing others into action. After all, Big Box was not going to be happy seeing its investment on the Stanford campus turned against it in a publicity disaster. They would pressure the administration to stop the protest or to at least minimize its impact. The group decided to risk it—go with Stanford but keep the planning for the protest as quiet as possible for as long as possible to minimize the time the administration would have to react.

Heavy argued that the location of the campus Big Box building—away from the center of the campus—was actually an opportunity, not a problem. They would gather at the fountain outside Memorial Hall. They could then march to the Big Box building and hold a teach-in there. Heavy loved marches. Always a good way to get the adrenaline flowing. At the Big Box building, they would have some speeches and make some demands for fixing Big Box—an end to corporate oppression, rebates to customers, higher wages for workers, a more sensitive corporate ethos and so on and on and on.

Getting ready for the march would take some work. They would need signs and banners and slogans. They would need to make the signs and banners so that they looked homemade but were still readable for the cameras that would certainly be there. Heavy would get the word out through his e-mail networks. There was much discussion of deconstruction and Western values, of symmetry and asymmetry of patriarchal and matriarchal structures and strictures. But before lunch could segue into dinner, they came to one more crucial decision. Ramon would be the main speaker, not some out-of-towner or big-name activist. Later, they could nail down the date for the protest and work on lining up other speakers.

It was almost four o'clock. Ramon went by Amy's place and she drove them to Baylands, a nature preserve that bordered the bay, at the end of Embarcadero. Near the entrance to the park was a pond. Amy and Ramon sat on one of the benches rimming the pond and talked. Around them, children and their parents fed the ducks and other birds that came to enjoy the water.

Amy told Ramon about her economics class earlier that afternoon. Her homework assignment was to come up with an example from the world around us that illustrates order that is not the product of deliberate design. As she told Ramon about the class and the homework, she noticed the ducks. She got a kick out of watching the delight of the children. But she didn't see the hidden order of the ducks and the children and their dance together, even though she and Ramon came often to this spot to unwind.

Somehow, there were always a lot of ducks to greet the children, but not too many. No one sent the ducks of the Bay Area a memo, inviting some this week, others the next. No organization monitored the duck arrivals and departures that assigned just the right number of ducks to this one little pond. Thousands on thousands of ducks in the Bay Area with thousands of square miles to choose from and somehow, just the right number of ducks—a few dozen rather than zero or a few thousand—would show up day after day.

No one ever marveled at how the numbers of children and the numbers of ducks matched so nicely. It wasn't perfect. Some days fewer children showed up than others. Some days, there were too many ducks fighting, competing for the food, and the children didn't have as good a time. But without a schedule or a scheduler, it worked remarkably well. But Amy was too focused on Ramon to see the hidden order that was at work around her.

Twenty feet from where Ramon and Amy sat talking, an ant colony bustled in response to the children and the ducks. The ants fanned out in search of crumbs too small for the ducks to notice. But the ants did not search randomly. When one ant discovered a collection of crumbs and returned to the colony, it left a trail of pheromones along the ground that encouraged other ants to take the same trail. So the colony acted intelligently, sending more ants to the spots with more crumbs. But no individual ant, not even the queen, knew this information. Amy did not see the organization of the ant colony.

On the surface of the pond were phyloplankton, too small for the eye to see. Their population fluctuated with the chaos of the temperature and the winds. A storm could flood the pond, keeping away the children for days, killing the ants but bringing in all kinds of nutrients for the life on the surface of the pond and below. The duck population, the ant population, the phyloplankton, the shrimp, the fish, the birds, and everything else created a web of life that responded to the forces of chaos with forces working toward order. The web of life linked the ducks to the shrimp and the shrimp to the zooplankton and the zooplankton to the phyloplankton that floated and drifted helplessly on the surface. The children added another set of strands to the complex web of life around the pond.

Amy was thinking of none of this. She was telling Ramon about Hayek, an economist she had learned about in high school. Hayek was interested in spontaneous order, order that sprung from the complex, unplanned interactions of individuals going about their business. Ramon was listening, but at the same time he was thinking about Amy and how the sun was now low enough to backlight her hair, how blonde her hair was and how beautiful it was in the light.

Despite the breeze that ruffled the surface of the pond, Ramon's body temperature rose ever so slightly from talking to Amy and looking at her hair. Not by enough for Ramon to notice even if he had tried, but a perfect thermometer would show that he was slightly warmer than he was when he first arrived. Ramon's body responded to the increase in temperature by radiating the extra heat into the evening air.

Amy and Ramon rose from the bench and walked to the entrance of the nature preserve nearby. The birders were out tonight with their field glasses and their tripods, but Ramon and Amy didn't notice them. Ramon and Amy passed through the Nature Center, then walked on a long boardwalk that took them out over the marsh to the edge of the bay. Swallows flitted about them as they walked slowly out over the marsh. At the end of the boardwalk was a small observation deck, a place to sit or stand and watch the shorebirds that seemed to be everywhere, rising and falling from the shallow water where the marsh caresses the bay.

Amy talked about Hayek and the paradox of how order can emerge without anyone being in charge. But deep down she was thinking about her future with Ramon and if it would be able to survive the end of life at school and the roads they were hoping to travel over the next five or ten years.

Amy told Ramon an example that she remembered from her high school class, that there are always enough bagels at the coffee shop on the corner and that you don't have to call in advance if you decide at the last minute to throw a brunch and it all happens without a bagel czar. Would that make a good example for her homework assignment, Ramon asked. No, she answered. That example was too close to the pencil story Ruth had told the class—how there are always pencils when you show up at the campus bookstore. Ramon asked Amy if something from biology might work. Something from the human body, maybe. There must be lots of self-organizing systems that made the body work so well. Yes, Amy said, the cell, the circulation of the blood, the heart.

At first, Amy didn't notice the small shadow that floated across the marsh. Ramon didn't see it either. They were both too engrossed in each other. But suddenly there was a rush of wings, something was happening just beyond their conversation and they both looked up as a hawk swooped down low over the marsh, looking to steal a quick meal from one of the nests in the thick marsh grass. But the marsh birds that were scattered over the water and hidden in the grass—the godwits, the avocets, and the black-necked stilts—saw the shadow. These birds thrive on slowness, taking so long to move forward one agonizingly slow step at a time that you sometimes wonder if they're really alive. But they reacted to the shadow as if an alarm bell rang announcing all crew to battle stations. An instant flock came to life. The birds rose nearly as one and moved toward the hawk, defending some territory only they knew of. The flock hovered for an instant and then accelerated toward the hawk. The hawk dove and tried to spin free, but the flock, filled with smaller birds, darted after the hawk as if they were a single bird on a mission, to catch the hawk or at least to drive it away. As the shorebirds danced after the hawk, moving this way and that, Ramon smiled and then laughed with the pleasure of it and turned to Amy, pointing to the mass of birds that ebbed and flowed in pursuit of the hawk. The rust-red wings of the godwits glowed in the orange light of the setting sun.

Amy followed the gesture of Ramon's hand. Ramon Fernandez was incapable of gracelessness. Amy's body temperature had been on the rise for the last few minutes. Without any conscious effort on her part, the slightest tinge of pink rose to where her cheekbones were closest to the skin, in that perfect curve below the eyes. Her upper lip dampened, glistening ever so lightly in the sunlight holding the remains of the day. As the hawk flew on, and the shorebirds returned to their still life, Ramon's gaze returned to Amy's face. Whether it was the change in color or the moistening of her upper lip or some other cause—Ramon could not explain it any more than he could explain the impulse of the shorebirds to defend their young so ably—Ramon took Amy in his arms and kissed her.

The sun was down now. Amy and Ramon went for dinner to a small Cuban place called Tito's at the border of Palo Alto and Mountain View. There were no pictures of Havana, no pictures of Hemingway, no atmosphere whatsoever. There were only the best black beans in the Bay Area. Ramon and Amy dressed up from their usual sweats and T-shirts to go there. Ramon put on a jacket. Amy wore a long, flowing skirt and a tight sleeveless top with a scooped neck.

After dinner, they went north to San Francisco, headed for a club near the waterfront. It wasn't in the nicest or fanciest part of the waterfront, the part that draws the tourists pretending they're on a wharf frequented by fishermen. The club where Amy and Ramon went was grittier, filled with people who actually worked on the boats and who hung out there to eat and drink and hear music after a long day of physical labor. The walls could have used a coat of paint. The bathrooms were merely functional. The only decoration over the bar was an old neon Cervesa Cristal sign. The focus was on the music and the dancing that went till one or two o'clock in the morning, even in the middle of the week.

Ramon and Amy should have been studying tonight, but the romance of salsa and mambo drew them northward. Five musicians were wedged into a corner of the club on a platform too small and inconvenient to call a stage. Older men, they played the classic tunes that attracted an older crowd. That alone would have made Amy and Ramon stand out. Ramon wore a fedora he found at a garage sale low on his head as a way of deflecting attention. Bringing Amy ruined that plan. Amy, blonde and close to six feet tall, was hard to ignore as they spun and flashed across the floor.

Ramon was dancing to music that was bred in the bone. Moving to its rhythms came without thought, like a child answering a mother's smile with one of its own. For Amy, it was an acquired taste. But she could hold her own. The two of them, Ramon and Amy, their bodies already perfect by themselves, looked even better moving together.

The lights were low and even those who recognized Ramon left him alone, giving him an island of peace to savor. Dancing to this music was a tonic of forgetting and remembering, forgetting the stress of tennis and school, remembering hanging out with his mother in their tiny kitchen in Miami, getting dinner ready, the radio always on, his mother humming and singing along. And there was a bit of imagining, too, imagining his father and mother dancing to these old tunes back in Cuba. Ramon could close his eyes, and the music, combined with the nearness of water, took him across the country, beyond the sea, to the island where he was born.

For Amy, it was a chance to get close to a part of Ramon that she only knew from conversation and Ramon's photographs. She knew something of his journey across the water as a boy, his mother's courage. She had seen the picture of Ramon, maybe five years old, smiling, wearing a cowboy hat, somewhere on the streets of Havana. A picture of his father,

barely older than Ramon was now, wearing a baseball uni-
form, the bat resting on his shoulder like there was a special
groove for it there and he carried it wherever he went. She
had seen the picture of Ramon's father and mother cruising
the Malecon, the legendary Havana boulevard by the sea.

But more than that? Ramon didn't talk much about Cuba
unless she pushed him. And she rarely pushed him. She knew
he had not been back. She knew Ramon's mother had not
been back and vowed not to return until Castro was gone.
Did Ramon have a similar vow? She didn't know. She only
knew that at least for now, he had no plans to return either
out of respect for his mother or for reasons of his own. She
only knew that nights like this were some way of connecting
with his youth, his father, with being Cuban.

What did his Cuban past mean to him? Amy could sense
something of an answer on nights like tonight, swaying and
sweating with the others out on the dance floor, with people
who could have been Ramon's aunts or uncles, marveling at
the dramatic gestures of their hands, the dignity and pride of
their heads held high, feeling the same music that was pounding inside them, watching Ramon's face in the dim light.

Tonight, both of them turned to the music for escape.
Ramon forgot about Heavy Weather, about Wimbledon,
about his classwork, about what would come after school as
his life unfolded. The music coursed through him like a river
and he moved to its current with no more effort than the
river on its way to the sea.

Amy worked harder than usual to lose herself in the
rhythms of the guitars and drums. She kept thinking about
this protest Ramon was getting entangled in. Or was he doing
most of the entangling? She couldn't tell yet, but she knew

enough about politics and the human heart to know that Ramon was taking a chance that might enhance or harm his image and career down the road. She saw no reason to trust Heavy Weather. She worried that it was a mistake, a mistake for Ramon, maybe a mistake for anyone.

"What's wrong?" he asked at the end of a song. "You look far away."

"No, I'm here," she answered.

She willed herself back into the music, moving in time to the ceaseless rhythm of the drums, moving in perfect union with Ramon, her skirt swirling like a white rose around his grace.

4

INCONCEIVABLE

Ramon and his mother Celia do as well as can be expected in their early years in Miami. At first, they sleep on the floor in the living room of a cousin. Within a year, the woman, who is working two jobs, has enough money to afford her own apartment. The boy is her only child, so the mother pours her time outside her working life into his future. She quits her second job so that she can spend more time with him. To make ends meet, she shops at thrift shops and finds new ways to cook beans with rice. She learns English so she can read to him. She learns English so she can help him with his schoolwork. She learns English so she can think of herself as an American. But at night, she tells him stories of his father and sings him to sleep with Cuban lullabies.

At Ruth's next class, Amy told how she had been at the marsh when the flock of birds had pursued the hawk.

"They darted and danced as if they had been programmed. No one in control, yet the flock had a life of its own. The wind is blowing and the hawk is moving, yet somehow, the flock held together. As if," and here Amy hesitated, searching for the right words, "it looked like the flock was under the control of a master puppeteer whose goal was to keep the birds flying together."

"A bunch of birds flying together," Ruth said, "is orderly, as opposed to a bunch of birds flying all over the place. But you got to see the real magic of the order that emerges—something happening that isn't the intention of the participants. That flock you saw last night appeared to have a goal—"

"To get rid of the hawk." Amy filled in the blank. "To move it away. But most of the birds in the flock were probably just trying to stay close together without running into each other. They followed simple rules and achieved something greater than just flying together."

"Great example," Ruth said. "Same with a school of fish. Or a herd of wildebeest being chased by a lion. And same with the pencil army. The graphite miner in Sri Lanka doesn't realize he's cooperating with the cedar farmer in California to serve the pencil customer in Maine. But they are working together like those birds. And they're responding to outside forces just like those birds. And they're achieving something that no one of them intends. It begins with the specialization. No one can make a pencil. The myriad of things you need to know to make a pencil is spread out all over the world. People specialize in a few tasks rather than having to master everything. That's good. Why?"

"You can get better and better at your task," Amy replied.

"That's right. By specializing, you acquire knowledge about the task at hand—how to mine graphite, how to smelt aluminum, how to grow cedar trees. Spreading out the tasks lets the most effective people for each of the many jobs acquire the knowledge they need to execute their part of the process. So far so good. That's the advantage of specialization. But there's a huge disadvantage."

"It gets boring doing the same thing over and over," Josh said.

"Yes. That's especially true for someone working on an assembly line, which is what we think of as specialization. But fortunately, these days, fewer and fewer workers have to work on an assembly line. We've found ways for robots and machines to do the most repetitive tasks. No, the real problem of dispersing the tasks is that you disperse the knowledge each of the participants has."

"Why is that a problem?" Josh asked.

"Sometimes you'll want that knowledge to be organized in some fashion."

"Isn't that what the pencil factory is?" Josh asked. "A knowledge aggregator? Does the pencil factory pull the knowledge together in the finished pencil by ordering from all the different suppliers with all the different kinds of expertise?"

"Yes," Ruth answered. "And it's a beautiful thing. But that knowledge, what we might call 'expertise' or 'know-how,' is only part of the knowledge that gets acquired because of specialization and then brought back together in some sense. Imagine if life were static and people wanted the same number of pencils year in and year out. And if cedar and graphite were only used in pencils. Each year, each supplier would just produce the same amount and get better and better at their tasks. But life isn't static. The number of pencils people want to buy isn't the same every year. And graphite isn't just used in pencils."

"Why is that so important?" Josh asked.

"Suppose carmakers figure out that graphite can be used in brake linings and will help the brakes work better. All of sudden, they want to buy a lot of graphite. But all of the current production of graphite is already being used. There isn't going to be enough graphite to go around. What happens next? What would we like to see happen? Should graphite suppliers go out and find enough extra graphite to satisfy the carmakers? Or maybe the other buyers of graphite—the pencil makers, the tennis racquet makers, the fishing rod makers, and so on—maybe they should cut back their purchases of graphite to free up enough for the carmakers. Or maybe the carmakers should compromise and use less than they'd like."

"Wouldn't it work out better," Andrea asked, "if someone were in charge to answer those questions? Why not take advantage of the human ability to communicate?"

"Do you think a flock of birds could do a better job if the birds could communicate and if one of the birds were in charge?"

"Sure," said Andrea. "Look at the Blue Angels. They're a flock of birds with communication. Five planes dance as one. But the birds can't quite manage that. There are always stragglers."

"True, the birds can't stick together with the efficiency of the Blue Angels. But all the swooping and turning of the Blue Angels is pre-planned. They practice the plan over and over again, until they get it right. Imagine the Blue Angels attacking a faster, stronger enemy plane, the equivalent of a hawk. Do you think the Blue Angels could swoop and move as one—attacking another plane that has the ability to improvise, the way a hawk can?"

"Impossible. They'd crash and burn."

"Chaos. But the Blue Angels can communicate. They have language. They have radios. But it wouldn't be enough. The birds have nothing but instinct. Yet they can stick together."

"That's bizarre. You'd think it would be better to have someone in charge to correct any mistakes."

Amy's mind wandered back to that evening last week out with Ramon—all those dancers, pairs moving as one, the woman following the man but each improvising along the way and no one controlling a couple's path across the floor. Even the man who was leading couldn't tell you where he was going to be in two or three seconds, yet somehow, none of the couples ever collided. There was some kind of order there, something like the flock of birds managing to fly together as one without crashing into each other. Somehow, the traffic on the dance floor managed itself, what you could call ordered chaos or chaotic order. Did anyone benefit from that spectacle of controlled abandon? The band, maybe, watching the couples swerving and swaying yet somehow staying clear of each other. That kaleidoscope of color and movement must fuel the fervor of their playing. It meant something to the dancers, too. The chaos of the dance floor created something that couldn't be matched by giving each couple a clean flight path in advance or its own circumscribed space on the floor.

Ruth's voice brought Amy back.

"You'd think having someone in charge could outperform the spontaneous dance of the birds. But only if that 'someone' could grasp all the knowledge each bird has, find a way to process that information, come up with a plan based on the information, and communicate the plan to all the participants quickly so they can do their assigned tasks before something else changes. Without that knowledge and without a way to communicate nearly instantaneously, the flock falls apart. The flock is smarter than the smartest bird in the flock because it has found a simple way to use the information within the flock, even when everyone is spread out and they have no formal way of communicating. Same with an ant colony—it looks like the queen or something or some-body is controlling everything. The colony finds a new food source and more ants head in that direction. A person walk-ing along steps on the ant hill and hundreds of ants mobilize to repair the damage. How does all that happen? You know the queen isn't using a cell phone to order people around. So how does it happen? There has to be some kind of simple feedback system that sends signals to the ants to get them to change their behavior."

"Why does it have to be simple?" Josh asked.

"Because the ants have very, very, very small brains. The whole thing has to be driven by instinct, a fancy word mean-ing we don't exactly understand what's going on. The ants use pheromones, chemicals they emit and leave behind. The pher-omones create the web of knowledge that allows the colony to respond to crisis or opportunity. The colony is smart even though every individual ant is oblivious to the big picture. The same thing is going on when there isn't enough graphite to go around."

"But we can use computers and other technology the ants don't have," Josh said. "We can communicate."

"True, but the biggest, fastest computers can't help you solve the problem. Let me make you the graphite czar, Josh. You have to decide how to hand out the graphite when car-makers suddenly start using graphite and there isn't enough to go around. Imagine getting all the people who use graph-ite into a giant room. There are the carmakers and the tennis racquet makers and the pencil makers. There are the drivers who are worried about making sure their brakes work well on a rainy night. There are world-class tennis players and weekend hackers. There are artists and first graders worried about pencils. There are the graphite miners and the people on land near those mines. All of those people and a few million I haven't mentioned all have a stake in who gets the graphite. But they also have a tremendous amount of knowledge we'd like to see the graphite czar use—that's you!—when you decide the best way to deal with the graphite shortage. The graphite miners have an idea of the best way to get more graphite and what that extra production is going to cost. The tennis racquet makers know how popular graphite racquets are compared to wooden ones. The pencil makers know whether they can mix more mud in with the graphite to make it go farther. So there's another connection between specialization and knowledge. The people who mine the graphite don't just know how to mine graphite. They also know about how to get more out of the ground quickly if it turns out to be really important. The tennis racquet makers and the pencil makers and the carmakers don't just know how to make their products. They know something about how to make them in different ways when circumstances change. Then there are the users. Some are almost as happy with a pen instead of a pencil. But there's an artist who wants twenty pencils today of all different kinds. And maybe people are really into tennis this year. Maybe the tennis racquet makers want to expand production. So maybe some of the users of graphite shouldn't cut back at all. They should get an increase. Having the world's biggest faster computer won't help you process the information that's in the minds of all the people who are affected by a graphite shortage."

"Why not?" Josh asked.

"Mainly because the answers aren't in a book or in Wikipedia. The answers aren't data that can be stored in some spreadsheet and manipulated. They're what the economist F. A. Hayek called 'the particular circumstances of time and place,' subtle knowledge that we might call ingenuity, the knowledge of how to produce more graphite quickly or where the extra trucks are going to come from that the graphite mining company is going to need to ship the graphite. The answer to that question isn't a number or even a place. It's probably different today than it was last month. And some of the knowledge gets produced through the process of coping with the increased demand coming from the carmakers. You're going to figure it out when you have to. That kind of knowledge can't be stored."

Ruth let them think about the idea of knowledge that wasn't storable. Then she continued.

"Even if you could interview all the buyers and sellers of pencils and tennis racquets and the graphite companies, and even if they could answer your questions, and even if they told the truth, you'd still have to weigh their competing desires—is the unpleasantness of having only six pencils instead of a dozen more important than the pleasure the new fan of tennis gets from a graphite racquet—and by the time you finally figured out how to hand out the scarce graphite and how much extra to produce, something else would change in the world to make your plan obsolete—a graphite mine collapsing somewhere or a few hundred million Chinese moving into the cities from the countryside, sending their kids to school for the first time and demanding pencils."

"I see it's hopeless," Josh said. "It can't be done."

"It can't be done but it gets done," Ruth said. "Weird, isn't it? No one answers those questions. But they get answered. A few hundred million Chinese have been moving from the countryside to the city. They're using more pencils. But have you noticed? Gone over to the bookstore for a pencil and been told sorry, but all the pencils have been shipped to China? Carmakers do use graphite in the brake linings. Looked for a tennis racquet but couldn't get one because the carmakers started using graphite?"

"No," Josh said.

"So how does order persist without anyone being in charge? How is it that the greatest migration in human history, the movement of the Chinese from the farms to the cities, has been so quiet? Why haven't we noticed? There should be lots of empty shelves. After all, there is no graphite czar. No pencil czar. No bicycle czar to make sure the Chinese moving to the cities don't buy up all the world's bicycles. No one's in charge."

Ruth looked around the room. The students were quiet, waiting for her to go on.

"Prices," Ruth continued. "Prices are key. The simple answer is that when there's a surge in demand for graphite from carmakers, the price of graphite goes up, encouraging other users of graphite to cut back. There isn't just a decree that everyone has to cut back 25 percent. The price increase encourages some users to stop using graphite entirely and to substitute something almost as good. Some users will find a way to use less. And some, because of something else is going on in another corner of people's lives, some will actually use more graphite, say because of that tennis fad or the Chinese migration to the cities. The higher price of graphite encourages the graphite mining company to look for new sources of graphite, sources that weren't worth seeking out when the price of graphite was lower. But it's really much more beautiful than that. If it's easy for graphite miners to find new supplies, the price doesn't go up very much, so all the existing users don't cut back very much. And if it's really hard for the existing users to find substitutes for graphite, then the price goes up more, encouraging suppliers even more and nudging carmakers to see if they can get by with less than they started asking for. Those are exactly the things you'd want to happen if there were a graphite czar, a graphite czar who had all the knowledge you could possibly imagine. But a graphite czar couldn't make it happen! How can it possibly happen without one?"

It was a rhetorical question. Ruth let it hang in the air.

"Prices steer resources around the economy," Ruth continued, "encouraging producers and consumers to cope with change in an extraordinarily orderly way. When prices rise or fall, they help buyers and sellers coordinate their actions in a way that could never be done from the top down. Changes in prices cause buyers and sellers to make decisions using the knowledge spread out all over the economy that no one person knows. And look at the result. No one fights over the graphite. Everyone gets along. Prices are the pheromones of the human ant colony we call an economy, the signals that hold the whole thing together, the tendons of the invisible hand. What prices achieve—the harmony and the implicit cooperation—is inconceivable. Inconceivable!"

"So the graphite suppliers set the price to make sure there's enough to go around," Andrea said.

"No, that's the wildest thing of all," Ruth said. "The graphite suppliers are trying to make as much money as possible. They don't have the knowledge necessary to set the prices to make sure there's enough to go around. No one has that knowledge."

"Then how does the problem get solved?" Andrea asked. "You told us that the prices use the knowledge you'd want used to make sure the right things happen. But surely, the graphite suppliers set the prices. And if the prices are doing what you say they do, the graphite suppliers must be making it happen. Aren't they?"

Ruth let the silence grow as she gathered her thoughts. The class waited. Ruth let the silence stretch a little longer to let them know that what was coming now was different.

"Suppose it's a cold day outside, below freezing, and your apartment is nice and toasty. Then you notice that it's getting warmer and warmer. What do you conclude?"

"My roommate probably turned the heat up," Eric said.

"Right. A no-brainer. Someone changed the thermostat. Someone wanted to change the temperature and that 'someone' did something about it. Human design followed by human action. And it's a no-brainer to figure out how to get the temperature back to a more comfortable range. What do you do?"

"You turn the thermostat back down," Eric answered.

"Right," Ruth said. "Now suppose you go out for a walk and it starts to rain. Who decided that it should rain? You might say, nature. Or God. But there's no person who made it rain. If you're a long way from home or if it's raining really hard, you might regret that you forgot to bring an umbrella or wear a raincoat. But you don't blame your roommate or anyone else. No one controls whether it's raining or not raining. Rain is a natural phenomenon. Or suppose you go for a five-mile run on a hot day wearing a heavy sweatshirt. You're going to sweat. Under the circumstances, sweating or not sweating isn't under your control. It's built into the system."

Ruth paused and looked across the room. She saw the students eager to find out what this had to do with the price of graphite or even just economics.

"Some things in life," Ruth continued, "are the product of human action and human planning or design or intention. Other things we experience have nothing to do with human action or design or planning. They are built into the fabric of the world, whether designed by God or simply part of nature, they are clearly not part of human action. It's easy to divide the world around us into two kinds of order: man-made and natural. But there's a hybrid category, a set of things in the world around us that are orderly as a result of human action but without human intention. An obvious example is language. Languages are alive. Who decided that it's okay to say something like 'I'll google her the next time I'm online.' Who made google a verb? Or xerox? Xerox—the company—tried to stop people from using xerox—the verb. But they couldn't stop it any more than the French government can stop people in France from saying 'le weekend' instead of the government-approved 'fin de semaine' to describe Saturday and Sunday. Who decided you can say 'can't' instead of 'cannot'?"

"Well, no one, I guess," Amy said.

"Exactly. But language isn't manna from heaven or even rain. It doesn't descend from on high. It's not of the natural world. It is clearly the result of human action. But it's not the product of human design. No one plans the English language or intends for it to take a particular form the way someone intends the temperature in the house to rise or fall. There's no dial to fiddle with. People try. So-called language experts or authorities try to influence how people talk. But no expert—and no committee either—decides how people talk. The way we talk emerges from the multitude of conversations we have with each other. Language is organic even though it doesn't grow in the ground. It's alive. It evolves. Some words catch on while others don't. But language isn't random. What emerges depends on what is useful. And words that are no longer useful, die. Hardly anyone says behoove, anymore. Or eleemosynary. They're dying, but no one killed them. 'We' killed them, but even that phrasing makes it sound like we made a decision. But it wasn't decided. The verb 'decided' implies intention and deliberation."

Ruth stopped here and let them absorb the lesson before continuing. What she was saying made sense, but they were waiting to see how she was going to tie everything together.

"Suppose it's late Saturday afternoon," Ruth went on, "five or six o'clock, and you want to drive into the city for dinner. How long does it take?"

"Forty-five minutes, maybe."

"How long does it take on a Tuesday night around the same time?"

"Longer."

"There's an orderliness—a predictability—to traffic. Driving on Tuesday at 6 p.m. takes longer than on Saturday. There's more traffic in the Bay Area than in Bakersfield. That might fool us into thinking that someone must be arranging things. Who decided that it should take longer on a Tuesday night compared to Saturday? Who decided that it should take longer to travel forty miles in the Bay Area compared to Bakersfield? Who sent out the memo telling more people to get on the roads at certain times and in certain places? Josh?"

"No one."

"No one. So whose fault is it that there are so many more cars on the road on Tuesday at six o'clock than on Saturday? It's no one's fault. But it's not an act of God or nature. It's clearly caused by human action, by human beings making decisions. But no one controls it. When you're behind the wheel going fifteen miles per hour in stop-and-go traffic, you're clearly driving the car. But surely it isn't your intention to go fifteen miles per hour. So why are you going so slowly? Why can't you go faster? We understand it's because of the other drivers. A Martian might think there's a car parade scheduled every day during rush hours where everybody decides to drive more slowly, but we know better. We understand that no one plans or intends for traffic to be slow during rush hour. But we still have trouble realizing that if we want to do something about traffic, there's no dial to adjust, no traffic thermostat. We want there to be. We expect there to be."

"No one driver can do anything about traffic. But we as a society can. We're smarter than the ants. We don't have to take the colony as it is. We can improve it," Josh said, looking into Ruth's face to see if it was okay to interrupt.

"Can we? How would we do that?"

"We can widen the road. Or spend money on mass transit," Josh answered.

"San Francisco has tried both. The 101 is wider than it once was. There's BART and CalTrain. Has it worked? Does it take less time to drive on Tuesday night? Is there less traffic in San Francisco compared to Bakersfield where the roads are narrower and there are fewer mass transit options?"

"No. But it helps, doesn't it?"

"For a while. But ultimately, the problem persists because widening the road or offering mass transit doesn't get at the underlying cause, which is that a lot of people want to live here—the weather's nice and the land is beautiful. Widen the road and you make it easier for people to live here. OK, we're almost out of time, but we're almost at the punch line. Suppose you own a house and you want to sell it. Do you get to set the price?"

No one wanted to answer. It sure seemed like the owner sets the price, but it was obviously the wrong answer. The room stayed quiet.

"OK, let's take my house here in Palo Alto. You know I'm retiring soon. I sit down with a calculator and I decide I need to sell my house and get $2 million to make sure I can live in a style I'd like to get accustomed to. So what do you think—is that a good price? Justin."

"I don't know, Professor Lieber. I've never seen your house. Never been in it. It might be a good price. It might not be."

"How would you decide?"

"I'd look at how big the house is, the yard, the neighborhood."

"And after you did all that, and you saw that similar houses were selling for $800,000, what would you say then? Do you think I'll get $2 million for my house if similar houses are selling for $800,000?"

"Probably not."

"Probably not? Maybe you'd like to go out on a limb. Take a chance."

"OK. People wouldn't pay $2 million for something if they could get something similar for $800,000.

"Why not?"

"A prospective buyer would be foolish to throw away $2 million buying your house when there are alternatives for less."

"Aha!" Ruth jumped up in excitement. "So who sets the price? Of course I'm free to write whatever number I want in the ad. I am free to put a price of $1 million or $2 mllion. Or $20 million for that matter, hoping someone will fall in love with something unique about my house. But if I want to sell the house, I better set a price close to the price of houses that are about as attractive as mine in terms of size, condition, and the neighborhood. Around $800,000."

"So who set that price?" Justin asked.

"No one. That's the price that emerges from the interaction of all the buyers and sellers of houses of similar quality, just like language emerges, just like travel time on a Tuesday night emerges. In the case of the house, price adjusts so that the number of people who want to buy a house of that quality, location, size, and so on, is roughly equal to the available supply. And here's how bizarre it is. No individual buyer or seller is trying to create an orderly housing market. Each buyer and seller is just trying to get the best deal. But the result is an order that no one intends. And the result of that order is that you can plan a move to Sacramento or San Francisco or Sausalito knowing there will be houses for sale. There's no housing czar. No one's planning to make sure there are enough houses in every market, given that people are constantly moving in and out of cities every day. But when supply and demand get out of whack, price adjusts, either up or down, and that in turn gives people the freedom to make their plans. Where are houses more expensive, Palo Alto or Des Moines?"

"Palo Alto," Justin answered quickly, happy to hit an easy one out of the park.

"So suppose you're trying to decide between two jobs, both with wonderful potential, one in Palo Alto and one in

Des Moines. You go out to Des Moines and find a house you really like for $150,000. Then you come to Palo Alto and my house is for sale for $800,000. Should you get mad at me for setting such a high price? Is it my fault? Whose fault is it? Who sets the price? I no more set the price of my house than I decide how fast to drive on the 101 during rush hour. We don't get fooled by rush hour. We know that even though your foot moves the accelerator, it's not your choice to go fifteen miles per hour during rush hour. And it's not the seller's choice to charge $800,000. No one sets the price. It emerges."

Ruth got up and began to pace in front of the class.

"Language," she continued. "The time it takes to drive downtown. The price of a house. The price of graphite. The price of a pencil. We create them through our actions but not intentionally. They are tapestries we weave unknowingly. They have an orderliness about them that no one intends. These are emergent phenomena, phenomena that are the result of human action but not the result of human design. When the result of an emergent phenomenon is a price, the phenomenon that produces the price is called a market. It's a lousy word, but I don't control what we call it. I wish I did," Ruth said, almost to herself. "The prices create order. They send signals to suppliers in the economy to expand or reduce what they're making. And that in turn gives buyers the freedom to change their plans and their dreams. People want to exercise more? There are suddenly new kinds of shoes, new kinds of clothes, new kinds of equipment to help them. Those new products emerge not because of some survey gathered by an exercise czar. The new products just show up in the stores. Quickly. Not ten years from when people want to get more fit. But almost on command. But we know there's no command because there's no commander. And as resources and people and energy flow into those new products, you might expect a sudden shortage elsewhere in the economy. But that doesn't happen either. All of our different plans and dreams somehow get woven together without disruption. It's almost magic."

Ruth went over to the window and stared out. Lost for a moment in thought, thinking how long she had been teaching economics and how long it had taken her to truly understand it.

"People think economics is just common sense, and some of it is," she continued. "But understanding what economists call a market—the phenomenon where price emerges and responds to the changing circumstances of life, the changing tastes and desires and creativity as new things get discovered—is not common sense. It's really the deepest thing that economists understand. It's the focus of this class—learning to understand this process that yields an unplanned, undesigned order without anyone controlling it. And all the consequences of that process—the specialization that emerges as a result, the knowledge that gets created and used as a result and how that process responds when you try to control it with regulation."

Josh raised his hand.

"It's nice that pencils are always available in the store," he began. "But some things are more important than pencils. Food. Health. Shelter. The basics. If you just let prices emerge, as you say, everything goes to the highest bidder. That isn't fair. The rich get the goodies and the poor get the leftovers. That's why it's important to go to the Big Box protest. We can't let them take advantage of people's suffering. Surely you'd agree, wouldn't you, Professor Lieber, that it's wrong to raise prices after an earthquake? You'll be at that protest, right?"

Ruth knew he was teasing her. She loved having him in the class. A class without someone like Josh was like chili without chili powder. She also noticed Amy blushing. Why was that, she wondered.

"What you're really saying, Josh, is that prices do more than steer resources around and let people use their knowledge. Prices also affect your happiness. It's true that anyone who wants to buy a house in Palo Alto is able to find one. But only at a very high price relative to Peoria. It's true that high prices after a hurricane make sure that people can buy milk if they want. But what if you're poor? What kind of freedom is there when you can't afford something? Is that what you're asking?"

"Yes."

"Hayek said that 'the curious task of economics is to demonstrate to men how little they really know about what they imagine they can design'," Ruth said.

"I'm sorry," Josh said. "What does that mean?"

"The protestors imagine they can change the price of one thing, say milk after a hurricane, and hold everything else constant. Presto. Cheaper milk. A better world. Who doesn't want cheaper milk? But the world isn't so simple. Let me tell you a story. My daughter Sara and my son-in-law Alan live in St. Louis. A few years ago, Sara was pregnant with their first child. Alan, bless him, is a bit of a worrier when it comes to childbirth. Actually, he's a total worrier. He's worried about the kid being healthy. He's worried about Sara being OK.

But his biggest worry is getting to the hospital. His biggest fear is delivering a baby in the car. He's worried about an earthquake on the way. Or a tornado. Or maybe a snowstorm, even though the baby's due in June. Or a snowstorm during a tornado. During a rush hour traffic jam. He's so worried, he even gets advice from the doctor on what to do if he has to deliver the baby in the car."

A couple of the students giggled.

"Couldn't agree more," Ruth continued, "though he's a prince of a husband. Anyway, Sara wakes up in the middle of the night—two, three in the morning—with undeniable labor pains. This is it. No doubt about it. Within a minute or two, Sara and Alan are racing down the stairs and jumping in the car. The car roars to life and almost simultaneously with the sound of the engine, Alan starts cursing. 'What's wrong!' Sara screams. She's going crazy because Alan never curses. She's totally panicked."

Ruth looked out the window, remembering that night.

"They were almost out of gas. The needle was on empty. E minus, actually. Sara bursts into tears. Alan lets loose a few more choice words. What should they do? The hospital is twenty minutes away, maybe fifteen miles. Can they make it? They decide not to chance it. They race to the nearest twenty-four-hour gas station, put in one gallon, and head to the hospital. They get to the hospital and a mere ten hours later,"—Ruth stopped and smiled—"Sara gave birth to a beautiful baby girl. Put yourself in Alan's shoes the night before. Your wife is in labor. You shoot out to the car, mind racing, trying to keep on top of everything. You see the fuel gauge. A million things go through your brain. How far is the hospital? How many miles? How many gallons do you need to buy? Which gas station should you go to? What's the quickest way to get there this time of night? Should you go to the nearest one given that you're going to head on to the hospital? A million things. But there is one question that does not go through your mind. And that is what makes the story worth telling. With all those thoughts going through your head, the one thing you don't worry about for a nanosecond is whether the gas station will be out of gas."

"Why would it be out of gas?" Josh asked. "They're never out of gas."

Ruth said nothing. She went over to the window and let Josh's statement sink in.

"That's exactly my point," she said finally. "The supply of gasoline is something you don't lose any sleep over. Somebody pumps it out of the ground, ships it on a tanker, refines it, trucks it all over the country, and the person who runs that gas station makes sure the station never runs out. Never. And someone also shows up for work at three in the morning at the twenty-four-hour station. You don't worry about that either. That long chain of chance is held together by self-interest. And it works remarkably well. Now, there may be things about the gasoline market you don't like. You may even think that buying and selling gasoline is nothing like selling houses because a few big players dominate the market. But there's no dial that lets you lower the price of gasoline without consequences. Most of you are what, twenty, twenty-one?"

They nodded.

"You weren't alive in 1973. Or in 1978. You missed the gasoline shortages of the 1970s. OPEC cut back on production and the price of oil went up. The government put a ceiling on the price of gasoline. Made it illegal to sell gasoline above a certain price. The ceiling reduced the incentive for retailers to sell gasoline and the artificially low price increased the amount of gasoline people wanted to buy. Sometimes, you'd show up at the station and there'd be a sign, 'Out Of Gas. Come Back Tomorrow.' Can you imagine? Probably not. But in those days, if you had to get to the hospital at three in the morning and found the needle on E, you might be out of luck. In those days, worrying about whether the gas station had gas would be the *first* thing you'd worry about. We had an energy czar in those days. A government official whose job it was to solve the problems of the energy market. The 1970s were the only time in my lifetime when you couldn't buy gasoline when you wanted it. Until a few years ago. When Hurricane Katrina hit the United States and destroyed a bunch of gasoline refineries, a group of attorneys general wanted to protect people from price gougers. So they imposed fines on anyone who charged 'too much' for gasoline. That made it risky for gas stations to charge what the market would bear."

"But that's compassionate. That's what government should do," Josh countered. "That's what the attorney general should have done after the earthquake the other day. It would have meant lower prices for all kinds of necessities."

"Maybe. After Hurricane Katrina, gas stations ran out of gasoline in the middle of the day. President Bush had to beg people not to buy gasoline unless they needed it. Begging doesn't work as well as higher prices to convince people to drive less and use less gasoline. The same sorry spectacle had already happened when flu vaccine was in short supply. The same compassionate attorneys general threatened any seller of vaccine with fines if they 'gouged.' So the price of vaccines stayed low. Lines formed as they always do when prices are held artificially low. Again, the president begged people to do without the vaccine if they had a lower risk of getting the flu. Some relatively healthy people surely listened and stayed away, but not enough. There were still lines. Old people waited in line for five, six, seven hours. Some collapsed and had to be hospitalized. One seventy-nine-year-old woman collapsed, banged her head, and died. She died!"

Ruth had been pacing. She stopped and faced the class.

"Here's the bottom line," she continued. "Prices do many things. Because prices change, there aren't persistent shortages. Prices marshal knowledge to cope with changes in circumstances. And prices transfer money from buyers to sellers. That last part is the easiest part to see—and we often aren't happy about it. But if you treat prices like a thermostat you can just dial down to make life easier for buyers, you will inevitably interfere with the other results that prices achieve. Know that there is no free lunch. Play with prices and you will bring disorder. You will lose the benefits of the flow of knowledge and resources that prices choreograph without a choreographer. And as we will see later in the course, even the buyers you are trying to help may be harmed by your efforts."

Josh started to respond but Ruth held up her hand.

"You're absolutely right about the protest, Josh," Ruth said. "Everyone from this class should attend that protest. Attendance is mandatory. And after you attend, I'd like each of you to write up an analysis of the economics of what you see and hear. We're out of time. See you next class."

5

LEANING ON THE GARDENER

The boy is five years old when she buys him his first baseball glove. He has been asking for it for a year. It isn't the money. She worries about the burden of being the son of the father. The boy spends his afternoons and all of his summer days at the little park at the edge of their neighborhood, playing ball for hours. Just like his father, he plays with boys much older than he is and holds his own. Most of the other boys are like him, born in Cuba and raised in Miami. They all know of his father and speak of him as if he were the patron saint of baseball.

One day, on the way home from the ball field, he sees a tennis coach giving lessons. He stops to watch. He is eight years old and looks ten or eleven. When the lesson is over, Ramon helps the coach collect all the balls scattered around the court and asks the coach if he can try the racket and hit a few. The coach, a local pro, says sure. The next day, Ramon returns and asks again if he can play. Soon, it is a regular unspoken arrangement. Ramon helps the coach. The coach begins to teach him the game.

Ruth Lieber wasn't surprised to get a phone call from Robert Bachman, class of '77, chairman and CEO of Big Box. A man who liked to control everything, even things he has no control over, calling someone who he thinks should have control over something she knows she can't control.

"Ruth? Bob, here." No last name. Just Bob. But he was right. She knew who it was.

"Bob! Great to hear from you. How are you?"

"Not as good as I was yesterday. I've got a little problem in the Bay Area and it's drifting awfully close to my favorite campus. The one you run."

A lot of people thought Ruth Lieber ran Stanford and that the chancellor's job was to raise money. When people would ask her what it was like to run the university, she would just laugh and talk about herding cats or, when she was in a more reflective mood, she'd compare being provost to being a gardener in a rain forest. You can't landscape the rain forest. You can plant here and there. You can prune here and there. But you don't run the rain forest. And you don't run a country or a university. You have an impact. You can nudge it in a particular direction. Maybe you can make a mark. You can't make it do what you want.

But wasn't she the CEO of academic life at Stanford? Wasn't she in charge? She would try to explain that the provost has to deal with tenured faculty and petty politics and the student body and the alumni. It's chaos without control. And Ruth knew enough CEO's to know that they can't really boss people around either. Leadership in any sphere requires motivating and delegating and sometimes letting things go.

Ruth smiled on the outside to keep her phone voice pleasant, pretending that Bachman was actually in the room, sitting across from her desk. For her, that was the hardest part of being a provost, smiling through insults or listening to fools or bullies. Bachman was no fool. Bachman had heard about the adventure over at the Big Box store in Hayward and now he'd gotten wind of the protest being planned for the Stanford campus. He wanted to know what Ruth was going to do to stop it. She danced around a direct answer. She spoke about her devotion to both academic freedom and Big Box, never mind that the two goals might conflict.

Bachman knew about dancing. After all the back and forth and professions of love and affection, Bachman reminded Ruth without a hint of subtlety of what was at stake. Surely Ruth was aware of Bachman's conversations with the Computer Science department and the Graduate School of Business to establish a new state-of-the-art information technology center focused on inventory control and just-in-time practices in the service sector. Surely Ruth was aware that a substantial gift, likely to be something between $30 and $40 million that Big Box was considering for the naming rights of such an interdisciplinary center was under discussion with the dean of the Business School, the chair of the Computer Science department, and the dean of Arts and Sciences. Surely Ruth was aware that disappointing those schools and the alumni working to make the Center a reality would be a disastrous outcome for both Ruth and Stanford.

"Yes, Bob," Ruth answered, stifling the urge to add, "I am not a moron." Instead, she said how much she appreciated the importance of the university's relationship with Big Box in general and Bob Bachman in particular.

"So what are you going to do?"

Ruth kept the phone a safe distance away from her ear for a moment longer to make sure Bachman was done yelling. She promised to talk to Ramon Fernandez. Evidently he was involved somehow. Yes, of course she knew him. He was already on her calendar, it turned out—he was part of the graduation ceremony and there was a meeting coming up to discuss the logistics. Would she promise to tell him he couldn't hold the protest? Didn't he need some kind of permit to hold the thing? Maybe. But a protest without a permit can be even more dangerous. Could she threaten to take away his scholarship? Work him over a bit with a baseball bat? Very funny, Bob, no, she couldn't promise any of those things. Yes, she would get back to him. Yes, she would stay in touch. Yes, she would stay on top of the protest. Yes, she understood the importance of doing something to keep Bob happy. Yes, she realized that $35 million, give or take a few million, was a lot of money. Yes, she understood the importance of Bob to the future of Stanford. Yes, yes, yes.

When the meeting for the graduation ceremony rolled around, Ruth paid more attention than she normally would have to Ramon Fernandez. She knew a little about him already, of course. His father was the legendary Cuban baseball player who had died young. His mother had brought Ramon to America in an adventure that had been a national news story for weeks. She had seen him play tennis. He was as intense a competitor as she had ever seen in a sporting arena.

During the meeting, Ramon was quiet and respectful, not at all what she might have expected from someone who was rumored to be plotting a protest of a key university patron. The seniors had chosen Ramon to be the student speaker at graduation, and the purpose of the meeting was to review the logistics and the plan for the day. When the meeting was over, Ruth asked Ramon if he could stay behind for a few minutes. He settled into one of the comfortable armchairs around a low table opposite her desk.

"Ready for Wimbledon?"

"I'm getting there." He was wondering why she had asked him to stay behind. Maybe she wanted some tickets. Or an autograph for a nephew or a granddaughter. He was used to this kind of attention.

"I'm sure you'll do well."

Ramon nodded, waiting for the request. When Ruth spoke again, it caught him by surprise.

"I hear you're planning a protest against Big Box."

Ramon didn't know what to say. He said nothing and waited for her to go on.

"I just heard a rumor," Ruth continued. "Just curious what you have planned."

Ramon stayed silent.

"I assume that you'll be making some demands. Can you tell me anything about them?"

Again, Ramon was bewildered. It was one thing for the provost to have gotten wind of their plans. But did she really expect him to tell her what they were planning to demand?

"If I were planning a protest," Ramon said finally, "I'd probably keep the details quiet. But I appreciate your interest." He smiled to try to defuse the situation.

"I enjoy protests," Ruth said. "But if I were you, I'd certainly demand that the university rename the building and give back the money it received for the naming rights. I'm sure you've thought of that."

Ramon was stunned. That was a great idea that he or Heavy Weather should have come up with. Big Box off campus! It was so obvious. They'd missed it. But this was nuts. The provost was giving him advice on how to embarrass the university. Was she crazy? Was he? Was he missing something? He decided to play along.

"Demands? Great idea. And how about a speaker? Who would you recommend?"

"You might consider—" and Ruth named a prominent author, a well-known antagonist of corporate America. "But to be honest, I find him a bit tiresome. A bit too full of himself. Good for the faithful but not so effective with the unconverted. I think you'd be the best speaker. You come from humble beginnings. That will be effective in going up against a big corporation. And you're local. People know you. They're crazy about you. They'll be rooting for you. And I heard from a friend of mine that you're almost as handy with a megaphone as you are with a tennis racket. You're the obvious choice."

What was going on here? How did Ruth Lieber of all people know that Ramon was planning to speak? Had it been a lucky guess? Had Amy talked to her? That was crazy. But the most interesting question was why Ruth Lieber seemed to be supporting the protest. Maybe it was a misdirection play—faking a drop shot and then lobbing the ball over his head as he raced to the net. Maybe she was trying to scare him or dissuade him. Or maybe it was the straight deal. Maybe she really didn't like Big Box at all. Ramon was pretty sure the Big Box money had come to the university before Ruth's time as provost. Maybe she thought it was a mistake. Maybe she was trying to embarrass her predecessor, who was now the president of the university. Then there was Amy. Amy was in Ruth Lieber's class. He had to talk with her. Maybe she'd have some insight into how Ruth felt about the protest.

"Be careful, Ramon. If you're having a protest, hypothetically speaking of course, I hope you're prepared for the unpredictable."

He looked at her and smiled. She seemed sincere. For a moment, this little woman sitting across from him reminded him of his mother. He had no way of knowing whether she was serious or not. So he simply nodded, told her he appreciated her advice, and went on his way.

The week of the protest, Heavy Weather and his Berkeley friends blanketed the campus with leaflets and posters demanding that Big Box get off the campus and that the university return the tainted money it had taken from the enemy of working people. Bob Bachman kept the pressure on from the other side, leaning on Ruth to produce results rather than mere words. He wanted to know what Ruth was going to do. Bachman demanded that Ruth shut the protest down or at a minimum, shunt it off to the side, off campus somewhere or at least not in front of the building that had his company's name on it. Was she going to let those kids embarrass him and his company without any consequences? Because if she was simply going to let matters take their course, then he would do something. If she did nothing, if the protest rolled forward as planned, then Big Box would make its own brand of trouble for Stanford. Not only would all future gifts be in jeopardy, but Big Box would sue Stanford for the money it had provided to name the Executive Education Center.

"But Bob," Ruth countered, as he badgered her in one of his frequent calls, just a few days before the protest was scheduled to take place. "You don't want to do that."

"I certainly do. And I will. Just watch me."

"But then you'll be playing right into the students' hands."

"How so?"

"I guess you haven't seen the leaflets that are all over campus."

"What about them?"

"They're demanding that Stanford give back the Big Box money and rename the building. If you take us to court and win, you'll be handing the students a victory on a silver platter. After legal fees, more like a golden platter. If you demand that Stanford give back the money you so generously provided for the Big Box Executive Education Center, we'd have to take your name off the building. And that would give the protestors the victory of getting you off campus. That would just encourage these kind of people to take it up a notch, if you know what I mean. You give them a PR victory like that and they'll be marching in Omaha, they'll be—" Ruth stopped. Bob Bachman had hung up the phone before she could explain why the best thing Big Box could do under the circumstances would be to double down, and make that $35 million donation for the IT center as a way of showing they would stand by their principles and not be intimidated by a bunch of kids who didn't understand the world of business.

The day of the protest arrived looking like any other Tuesday in April on the Stanford campus. Temperature in the seventies, blue sky with a few clouds. If Bob Bachman had been hoping for rain, he was to be disappointed.

The crowd gathered at the fountain outside Memorial Hall and began the march across campus toward the Big Box Executive Education Center. Heavy Weather was in his element, handing out signs and banners he and his friends had made. He was so glad it was Big Box they were taking on and not Home Depot. How do you satirize Home Depot? What's a Depot anyway? But the box motif was delicious and perfect for the TV crews that were documenting the whole affair and making sure that Bob Bachman could watch the highlights on the news that night, even in Hong Kong where he was visiting some clothing suppliers. On the march, there were big boxes and little boxes. Boxes with slogans. Boxes like little coffins for the kids starved by Big Box's greed the night of the earthquake. Kids starved by Big Box's low wages. Boxes set on fire. Boxes on sticks with posters underneath. Boxes as clothing for naked marchers who couldn't afford to buy clothes because of Big Box price gouging.

The Big Box Executive Education Center was a marvel of cedar and glass. It made an exquisite backdrop for Ramon's speech, and Heavy had told all the camera crews in advance where to take their positions in order to get both the podium and the building in the same shot. Rarely had the hosts of a protest site proved so friendly. Ramon had been able to convince the administration that this was a learning opportunity and they had kindly provided the podium and a sound system. Suckers, thought Heavy Weather. They're all a bunch of suckers.

Amy marched, her devotion to Ramon overwhelming the doubts that studying economics with Ruth Lieber had planted. Ruth was there, too, though she didn't mingle with the crowd. No sense in giving Bob Bachman any additional unpleasantness in case the camera caught her in the middle of things. She hung back from the main event, content to watch the march and catch Ramon's speech over the loudspeakers from a distance.

Ramon's speech was masterful. It began with a recounting of the night of the earthquake. He talked about the injustice of exploiting the poor by jacking up prices during emergencies. He demanded that Big Box pledge to keep its everyday prices low every day. His plan was to reprise his speech of the earthquake night with a little more intensity. This time, he would use the crowd as a tool at his command. He would explain the heartlessness of Big Box's pricing policy, bringing it home with the story of the Mexican woman and her plaintive cries for her children. He expected that it would have the same effect on this crowd as it had that night. But instead of riling up the crowd and then defusing it as he had that night at Hayward, today he would channel that emotion and lead it.

Heavy and his cadre from Berkeley would start a chant of "Big Box Must Go." They would march to the administration building and with the cameras in tow, pile up all their boxes and signs and block the entrance. There they would unfurl an enormous banner, saying "Big Box Off Campus," and force the members of the university administration to tear through the banner if they wanted to get into their offices the next morning. This last part of the plan was a secret—only a handful of the planners knew how things would go. But they were confident that the natural emotion of the crowd would lead them to follow and march on the admin building. It would be a piece of cake, Heavy had explained. The world was full of sheep and a crowd was just a herd of sheep waiting for a shepherd. Heavy would lead them once Ramon had set the tone.

All eyes were on Ramon, but he was totally relaxed. He had been in the camera's eye many times. His command of the situation was absolute. Heavy marveled at his presence. He had never had such an extraordinary accomplice in protest theater—a world-class athlete who could turn a phrase, capture the crowd with his narrative, and pull the whole thing off with panache. Too bad he was such an idealistic kid. And Ruth Lieber, watching the whole thing unfold before her, had an entirely different vision, one that would change the world in one of those moments of electric reality when the path that events will take suddenly becomes transparent, as if the entire concept of time is meaningless and the future is no more unknown than the past.

Ruth, Ramon, and Heavy Weather. Each one thought that the situation was under control, but only one of them was right. The other two were simply amateurs, looking at what is seen and missing what is unseen. Ramon finished his story of the Mexican woman, and the crowd began to chant on cue, "Big Box Must Go!" Ramon descended from the platform to join the chanters and lead the group to the admin building. But he didn't get far. Suddenly the crowd surged around him, buffeting him and pushing and shoving. He began shouting to turn them around, desperately trying to stem the tide, but he barely heard his own voice in the chanting of the crowd. They surged past the podium, heading in the opposite direction from the admin building, surging toward the Big Box building, and just before he fell, Ramon's extraordinary peripheral vision gave him a glimpse of Heavy Weather in the lead, stooping down to pick up one of the stones that landscaped the space in front of the building. Smooth and cool in Heavy's hand, the shape and heft of the stone were perfect. Ramon fell before Heavy flung the stone, but his throw, the first of many, was captured on film by the news teams. Hundreds followed Heavy's lead and in a few moments, the whole front of the Big Box Executive Education Center simply disappeared in a cascade of shattering glass.

Twenty miles away, fifty protestors in front of the Big Box store in Hayward duplicated the feat. The camera crews were there, too. Heavy had called them all in advance, for if it isn't captured on film, has it really happened? The choreography was complete.

Amy was swept up by the crowd into the group that threw stones. She had no more control over her path than a piece of loose seaweed in the ocean tide. Ruth was far enough away to watch with enough dispassion that when she saw the surge toward the building and the stone-throwing begin, she was able to stifle her urge to use her cell phone and bring the campus police. They would arrive soon enough. By the time they were on the scene, the stone throwers were long gone. Instead of arresting anyone, the police helped the fifteen or twenty people who had been knocked to the ground by the buffeting of the crowd or who had been hit by stones that missed their mark. One woman sat dazed, blood streaming from a cut above her eye. Her face would be on the front page of every paper in America next to the shattered façade of the Big Box Executive Education Building.

And Ramon? Where was Ramon? Ruth saw him limping toward the gym.

6

Mea Culpa

When Ramon is twelve, he wins the toughest fourteen and under tournament in the city. When he almost wins the top regional tournament for fourteen and under in Atlanta, representatives from the tennis academies from around the state come calling at the Fernandez house, offering scholarships and selling promises of greatness for Ramon. Some of the men who stop by find themselves as interested in the mother as they are in the son. She is only a little over forty and still a beauty. Her brother Eduardo tells her it doesn't hurt to be nice. She is nice but nothing more. She thinks of herself as Penelope, but a storm has wrecked the ship of Ulysses and he has drowned. She chooses the tennis academy in Miami with the best academics that will let Ramon live at home.

After Ramon wins Junior Wimbledon in his junior year in high school, the universities with the best tennis programs in America begin writing letters, sending brochures, and inviting Ramon for a visit. He decides on Stanford. His freshman year is near perfect. He loves the university, loves the tennis program, loves his classes. In the spring, he wins the NCAA singles championship. It's time to turn pro. He'll be able to move back to Miami and buy his mother a house. But she says no. She tells him her apartment is just fine. It's what she's used to. She makes him promise to stay in school all four years.

There's no limit to what you can accomplish if you don't care who gets the credit. This maxim, attributed to every successful leader since Moses, often entered Ruth Lieber's consciousness in her job as provost. It was at the front of her mind, two days after the Big Box protest, as she sat listening to Bob Bachman lecture her about how lucky she was that everything turned out OK.

Part of Ruth Lieber's job was to make someone who thinks he's very important, feel even more important. This wasn't easy, but she did the best she could. She praised Bob Bachman on his foresight and yes, she admitted, it did turn out OK, thanks to a bit of luck. Yes, the protestors had carried some nasty signs and that tennis player had said some nasty things. But the overall impact had turned out remarkably well. The destruction of the glass front of the Big Box Executive Education Center had turned public opinion against the protestors and made Stanford look like the victim of vandalism rather than a partner in exploitation with its corporate benefactor. The damage to the Hayward store had generated sympathy for Big Box and led to further dislike of the protestors. Television crews caught people arriving at the store only to discover that the store was closed for repairs, thanks to the efforts of Heavy Weather and his friends. In one news story, Ruth told Bob, an interviewed shopper even compared the protest to the earthquake—in both cases, you couldn't get what you wanted. All in all, a very satisfying turn of events, even if it had all been a matter of good fortune.

At least, that's what she told Bob, because there was no way she could explain how she let the events unfold the way they had to, in the only way that would end up being good for both Stanford and Bob Bachman. Unfortunately, it meant tarnishing the reputation of a prominent Stanford student having him involved in such a destructive and violent event, but he will have better days, she thought to herself. A moment of idealism gone wrong will be forgotten. And she did warn him. Or so she told herself.

Only the end of the conversation raised a warning flag.

"And the best thing about how events turned out," Bachman crowed, "is the end of that Fernandez kid. He can go back to what he does best. Playing tennis."

Ruth didn't tell him that Ramon Fernandez could still cause Big Box plenty of trouble. With the weapon of a graduation speech still coming up, Ramon had one more chance to bloody Bachman's company. But Ruth figured that was still weeks away. Who knew what Ramon Fernandez would talk about? No need to make Bachman nervous about one more problem he would only pressure Ruth to fix. If Ramon Fernandez stayed on safe topics and there were no further Bay Area embarrassments for Big Box, she was pretty sure that Bachman would come through with the $35 million for the IT center. Then the intercom rang.

"Ruth, Ramon Fernandez is here to see you. Can you squeeze him in?"

"Sure."

Ramon entered and they sat in the same place in her office they had before, at the sitting area by the window, away from the desk.

"How's your leg?" Ruth asked.

"Better. How did you know?"

Ruth waved her hand and Ramon was reminded that he had underestimated the little woman sitting across from him. He put it all out of his mind, his leg, her apparent omniscience, his discomfort at being in her office after all that had happened.

"I owe you an apology," Ramon said. Ruth started to correct him, but stopped herself. She let him go on.

"You tried to help me," Ramon continued. "You warned me that I might be in over my head. I ignored you. Thought you were kidding around with me. Or trying to trick me. You were right. I was wrong."

She liked the way he said it. Straight, no chaser. No excuses. No mumbling. His eyes fixed on hers. When he got older, he was going to be some kind of person. He already was, she realized. He already had a presence about him that would take him wherever he wanted to go. In tennis or anywhere else. He was a little naïve, yes, but he would overcome that soon enough.

"I embarrassed myself," Ramon went on. "But more than that, I embarrassed the university. I'm sorry for that. And I wanted to thank you for trying to save me from making a mistake."

For a moment, Ruth thought of smiling and saying she appreciated him coming to see her and that she was looking forward to hearing him speak at graduation. Her desk was cluttered with work that needed to get done today. She had to teach her class. Her calendar was full until a dinner at eight that would run late into the evening. She didn't have time to talk to Ramon Fernandez. Had she simply thanked him and sent him on his way, she would see him again once or twice before graduation and that would be it.

But some instinct told her to take a different path from the obvious one. And so she changed his life and her own in ways she could never have predicted. Ruth looked back at Ramon and, given what she was about to say, she knew that his naivete, which had already taken a hit from Heavy Weather, was about to take another from her.

"You don't owe me an apology. And you don't owe me your thanks, either."

Ramon looked puzzled. What could she mean?

"It was a no-lose proposition for me," Ruth continued. I warned you so my conscience would be clear. I'm not proud of it."

Ramon still had no idea what she was talking about.

"As the provost, I had to worry about the reputation of Big Box. They're a major donor to this university. And they have the potential to become the biggest, actually. If the protest had led to a prolonged PR disaster for them, then it would have damaged our relationship. And I had to worry about the university as a whole. What would a big splashy protest mean for our national and international reputation? And I had to worry about you. I didn't want you embarrassed or looking foolish. So I warned you. But by warning you, I was serving my other goals as well. If you had bowed out of the protest, it would have lessened the damage to Stanford and the Big Box relationship because it would have been the work of outsiders. But if you stayed involved, I needed you to take an extreme position as you did, the position of pushing Big Box off campus. I know the CEO of Big Box pretty well. I knew that if you pushed the demand of Big Box off campus, then that would actually push Big Box and us closer together."

"So why didn't you just cancel the protest?"

"If I canceled the protest I would have created sympathy for the protestors. That would have hurt Big Box. And I would have lost any hope of influencing events in a way that might turn out to the benefit of the university. I was happy to let the protest unfold as long as it unfolded in a way that wasn't too harmful. After I gave you the warning to watch out, I sat back and let events take their course. I figured the incentives were in my favor."

Ramon leaned forward in his chair.

"But what about justice?"

"Justice?"

"You were worried about the university. You were worried about Big Box. You were worried about the relationship between Big Box and the university. You even worried a little about me. But what about justice? Didn't you worry for a moment about what was right and what was wrong?"

How could she sleep at night knowing she manipulated the situation to help a social parasite like Big Box, Ramon wondered. She seemed like a decent sort. Was it just to get more money out of them down the road? How could she live with herself?

Ramon was transformed. When he had entered her office, he was humble and subdued. Now he was on fire, his eyes the eyes of the competitor that she had seen on the tennis court. She let the emotion blaze for a moment, enjoying the passion. She stood up and looked out the window to let him calm down. Then, instead of answering his question and justifying her behavior, she answered his question with one of her own.

"So where would you rather shop?"

He had no idea what she was talking about.

"What do you mean?"

"Where would you rather shop? At a Big Box or a Home Depot? At a store that doubles its prices when there's a catastrophe or a store that leaves its prices unchanged?"

"That's easy. At a store that leaves its prices unchanged." Ramon wondered what she was up to, other than ducking his question and avoiding confronting what she stood for.

"So where did you shop that night of the earthquake? At Home Depot or at Big Box?"

Ramon saw where she was headed, now, but he still didn't understand.

"I shopped at both."

"Did you buy anything that night?"

"I was with a friend. We went to Home Depot first, but they were out of flashlights. So we ended up at Big Box."

"So where was there more justice? Big Box or Home Depot?"

"Home Depot. They didn't try to rip us off."

"But they also didn't provide you with what you wanted. Big Box had what you wanted. Is it possible that they were doing the right thing and the other stores that left the prices unchanged weren't?"

"But Big Box had flashlights and milk in stock for the wrong reason. It had nothing to do with justice or what was right. They were just trying to make a profit. They should have left their prices unchanged. That would have been the right thing to do."

"Did you ever wonder if the reason they had the milk and flashlights available was precisely because the prices were high?"

"I don't care. It's the wrong way to do things."

"Maybe. But think about the mom you helped."

"How—"

"I read about it in the paper. The story said you collected some money so she could afford stuff for her kids."

"It was outrageous, ripping off a mom shopping for baby formula and diapers."

"Maybe. But it was late at night. Think about the people who came through the store earlier, who might have stocked up on baby formula but decided not to when they saw those high prices. The high prices got them to step aside and leave behind some of those supplies for that mom. Some people came to that store thinking it would be nice to have extra diapers or an extra flashlight or extra batteries. But at twice the usual price, some of them—not all of them—but some of them decided to pass. That left stuff behind for you and the woman you helped. Is there any justice there?"

"No. When you use prices and let corporations gouge, the rich will still buy what they want and the poor will get stuck with the dregs. That's the way the system's designed."

The intercom buzzed. Ruth glanced at her watch.

"Sorry. I wish we could keep talking. But I have a meeting. But can I ask you one more thing?"

"Sure."

"On the night of the earthquake, there aren't enough flashlights to go around. At the usual, everyday prices, people want to buy more flashlights than there are flashlights on the shelves. Agreed?"

"Yes."

"So here's my question. Given that there aren't enough flashlights to go around, who should get them?"

"That's easy. The people who need them the most. Not the people who already have one. Not the people who have lots of candles. Not the people who are going to sleep most of the night anyway."

"OK. So how do you make sure that the people who need them the most are the people who get them? The problem is really one of knowledge. How do you find out who really needs the flashlights? That's not a trivial problem. You can interview people all night and in the morning give the flashlights to the people who you decide made the best case for why they deserve a flashlight. Is that a good plan?"

"I don't know. I'm not sure people would tell the truth about why they need one."

"Good. And you have to worry about more than just flashlights. You have to decide who gets the milk and the beer and the candles and the diapers and the portable generators and the thousands of things that people suddenly want in an emergency. If you leave the prices alone at their regular everyday levels, then who gets the flashlights and the milk and the generators?"

"The people who need them."

"I don't think so. If you leave the prices alone, the people who get the flashlights are the people who get there first. When you went to Home Depot, the stuff you wanted was already gone. But at Big Box, anyone who wanted a flashlight could have one."

"If they were willing to pay for it. That made it harder on poor people. Like the mom I helped."

"Agreed. But for thousands of people, there were flashlights waiting for them. Remember that knowledge we wanted to have? The knowledge about who needed the flashlights the most? When Big Box raises the price of flashlights, someone who had candles at home decided to do without the flashlight and left it there for you on the shelf. No one had to interview either of you. The higher price induced both of you to act as if you had been interviewed. The person with the candles, by refusing to buy the flashlight at the higher price, was saying, I'll pass on buying a flashlight. I'll leave it for someone else who needs it more. But no one begged him to do the right thing or passed a law that would have to be enforced or interviewed him to find out who needed it the most. The higher price made sure you got the flashlight. That seems pretty just to me."

"Maybe." Ramon was softening a bit. It was an interesting point. It reminded him of something, something that Amy had told him about her class with Professor Lieber, something about pencils and how prices use dispersed knowledge. "But it's unjust for Big Box to profit from my distress."

"Are you sure? Do you feel better about Home Depot? They didn't profit from you. But then again, they didn't save a flashlight for you, either. And when the next earthquake comes, which store has the incentive to order plenty of flashlights and milk and bear the costs of having more stock on hand, not knowing for certain whether the money spent will be wasted if the earthquake doesn't come? Big Box or Home Depot? Knowing they can charge a higher price gives Big Box the incentive to bear those inventory costs."

"But I want a world where flashlights are both cheap and available! Why can't we have both? Why do the rich keep getting richer and the poor, at best, are stuck climbing uphill? You're the economist. Tell me why we can't do better."

The intercom buzzed again and Ruth had to ask Ramon to leave. As he walked across the quad, he admitted to himself that Ruth had made some interesting points. But wasn't the whole thing a way to defend her corporate patron? How could it be compassionate to punish people in an emergency with high prices? She was a smart lady. He gave her that. A formidable adversary. And why had she been so honest with him? It was like being invited by the cook to see the kitchen of a restaurant you liked.

She hadn't said anything about his graduation speech. After the protest, he assumed she'd find a way to push him off the program. But she'd done nothing, yet. As far as he could tell, it was still on. So why had she told him the real story behind her conversation with him and how she had manipulated events? It would be awfully embarrassing if he told people about it. He shrugged it off as a mystery.

"So how'd it go?"

Amy was waiting for Ramon at the big fountain outside of Memorial Hall. He loved the spot. Somehow, the sound of all that cascading water opened his mind.

"I don't get it," Ramon answered. "I don't get her. She tried to tell me that it was a good thing that Big Box doubled its prices that night!"

"Did she say anything about cookies?"

"Cookies? Cookies. No she did not say anything about cookies. Why would she?"

"It was a homework assignment. When a mom only has two cookies to share among three children, should she auction them off to the highest bidder?"

"That's ridiculous."

"We all agreed. So Professor Lieber asked us to come up with other options."

"That's easy. She can give each kid two-thirds of a cookie. Or maybe she knows that one kid had a candy bar for a snack that afternoon, so that kid can do without the cookie. Or one kid can offer to be nice and let his brother have one. Don't tell me that the provost auctioned off cookies to her kids when they were little."

"It does sound like something some economists might do. But in Professor Lieber's case, I don't think so. Her point was that a parent has the knowledge to figure out who can go without a cookie. Sometimes, kids will share. There's no need to use prices. Same thing in a small town. In a small town, in an emergency, most of the citizens do the right thing either because they care about each other or because being selfish when there's a crisis is going to have costs—people might shun you in the future. So when there's an earthquake in a small town, the hardware store owner doesn't raise the prices of the portable generators. And even if they sell out, someone who desperately needs one can probably find one to borrow. But in a big city, there isn't as much love or knowledge to go around. Higher prices substitute for the lack of love. They encourage people to step aside and let strangers who are willing to pay the higher price, get the goods. And higher prices give business people an incentive to stock up on crucial items and bear the costs of inventory." "So what do you think?" Ramon asked.

"About what?"

"About Big Box doubling its prices. You weren't happy that night. You make it sound like they did the right thing."

"I see the good and the bad. High prices are bad for really poor people who need stuff. But they're good for people who need stuff, even some poor people, because the stuff's more likely to be there when they go to the store. And they're good for people who are going to need the stuff the next time there's an earthquake. Maybe you have to take the bad to get the good. I don't know. You?"

"I want a better way. It's hard to believe that the way we do things now is making the world a better place. It seems to me we ought to be looking for ways to make a big city more like a small town. What would Ruth Lieber say to that?"

"I think she'd say what she usually says in class. It's not enough to want to make the world a better place and it isn't enough to do something that looks like it makes the world a better place. The goal is to actually make the world a better place. And that is often a lot harder than it looks. Ask Heavy Weather."

"I'll pass. But point taken."

Back in the admin building, Ruth finished her meeting and looked over some notes for the next one. She went over to her calendar and looked at the next few weeks. If anything, the next few weeks were busier than usual. She really didn't have the time to spare. Should she risk it? The costs were clear. The benefits, a wild roll of the dice with a very high variance. They could even be negative. So what to do? The chairman of the Physics department liked to tease her, saying that if you laid all the economists in the world end to end, they still wouldn't reach a conclusion. But Ruth Lieber, the quintessential economist, had managed to reach a conclusion after all.

7

The Goose That Lays the Golden Eggs

Cuba is frozen in time, and that time is the early 1960s. The stucco walls of the capital are like a giant sand castle slowly eroding with the tides. Even the cars are from the 1960s. They prowl the streets like dinosaurs, waiting for an ice age to put them out of their misery. Everything is as it always was. No one expects it to be any different tomorrow.

Few revolutions keep their promises and the Cuban one is no exception. How much is the fault of the American embargo and how much is the fault of the hubris of Cuba's great leader is a matter for the historians to sort out. Who knows? The truth is elusive, but the Great Leader's blunders are famous among the people, though they are spoken of only in whispers.

Go out into the countryside and you can see a bridge that crosses a river without a road to follow on the other side. The goats use it to cross the river when the rains make it difficult. There are the coffee bean plants ringing the city that were going to make the nation a coffee powerhouse. Maybe the soil is too acidic or not acidic enough. Maybe there is too little rain or too much. Whatever the reason, there is no coffee bean harvest to speak of.

And then there are the prisons. Can there be political prisoners in the worker's paradise?

Early one May morning on the Stanford campus, only a few people were even awake. But at least one was not only awake, but working. He took the fuzzy ball in his left hand. He cradled it for a moment, then hoisted it up and flipped it into the air higher than you'd think he could possibly reach. But he could reach it. He brought the racket up and over the ball with a deceptively languid motion. Boom. Somehow, the campus managed to sleep on. Another ball. Up. Reach. Boom. Then another and another and another.

He did this for forty minutes. Then he retrieved all the balls, put them with the racket in the bag. He took out a towel and sat at the bench next to the referee's chair. Just before 8:30 in the morning and it was still quiet. Blue sky up above, everywhere else was evergreen, that deep green of tennis courts and the green seats surrounding him in the tennis stadium. He was alone, but if he closed his eyes, he could see and hear the fans filling the seats. How many matches had he played here? A hundred? Something moving caught his eye. He looked up and saw Ruth Lieber coming down the steps onto the court.

"I thought I might find you here," she said, sitting down next to him. Ramon began toweling off, drinking a blue PowerAde. What was the provost doing at the tennis complex at 8:30 in the morning? Looking for him, was the obvious answer. But why?

"Time here goes by so quickly, doesn't it?" Ruth asked.

"Yes it does. That's what everyone says. And they're right. So what's up, Professor Lieber?"

"Not much. I just wanted to continue our conversation from yesterday."

Ramon couldn't imagine why. But he needed to cool down anyway before running some sprints. He was happy to listen.

"Fine by me."

"Something you said yesterday, I can't get it out of my mind. You said something like the rich get to buy what they want and the poor get the dregs. Was that it?"

"Yes. Something like that."

"You asked me why we can't do better. So how do you think we're doing right now? Is the average person making progress? Is the standard of living of the average American higher or lower than it was a hundred years ago?"

The question didn't help Ramon figure out why this little woman had come out early in the morning to talk to him. She must have something on her mind besides America's standard of living. Probably trying to influence his graduation speech through some scheme. Well, let her scheme away. She was interesting to talk to. No harm there.

"I don't know," he answered. "Some people are wealthier. Some are poorer. But I'd say the average is higher, I guess."

"You're right. So how much higher do you think it is compared to 1900? A little higher? A lot higher? Ten percent higher? Twice as high? Give me a ballpark guess."

"Maybe 50 percent higher?"

"Well, you're close."

"I am? It was just a guess."

"You're close to what most people answer when I ask them. They usually say something between 50 percent and 100 percent. Though some say 10 percent and some think we're actually worse off."

"Is that close to the right answer?"

"There's no right answer. But some answers are better than others."

"Explain."

"In theory, the answer is easy to find. You look at average or median income in the United States today and compare it to 1900."

"Sounds pretty easy. But prices are higher today than they were a hundred years ago. So how do you adjust for that?"

"You have to either adjust the 1900 incomes upward or the current ones downward. The problem is figuring out how much the adjustment should be. Do you have a music player?"

"Sure." He reached down into his gym bag and showed it to her, the latest iPhone from Apple—phone, radio, television, GPS, and yes, a music player.

"What did you pay for it?"

"I think it was $139."

"OK. So if you earn $7 an hour, it takes twenty hours to buy one, or a little over two days of work. Do you like it?"

"What, the player? Sure. It's fine."

"What would you do to make it better? Closer to perfect."

"More storage capacity. Better headphones. Longer battery life. Quicker download time."

"So let's say in a year, you're making $14 an hour and your player is now $280. Has it gotten cheaper or more expensive?"

"The same. It takes twenty hours to earn one."

Right. But suppose the new one holds four times as many songs, has three times the battery life, and comes with a microwave oven."

"You're kidding about the microwave, right?"

"I am. But even without it, it's a much better player but twice the price. Has it gotten cheaper or more expensive or is the price the same?"

"The price in money is higher. The price in time is the same. But it's not the same player, really."

"Exactly. In some fundamental sense, the new player is cheaper. And suppose you want to compare your standard of living today with someone's from thirty years ago. What was the price of a digital music player thirty years ago?"

"There weren't any. How do you deal with that?"

"Not very well. You have to compare it to a portable CD player or maybe a cassette player. An even bigger apples and oranges problem. But how about one hundred years ago? A hundred years ago, the only portable music option was to hire a violinist to walk around with you. So comparisons of standard of living over a century, and sometimes even over decades, are inevitably crude."

"So how do you correct for those changes over time?"

"You make some assumptions about how many apples it takes to make an orange. When you're done, you've got what an economist would call an 'estimate.' That's a fancy word for a guess. Some guesses are better than others."

"So give me a decent one."

"A good guess is that we're somewhere between five and fifteen times better off in terms of material well-being than we were one hundred years ago. Maybe more."

"Wow. But it's not a very precise guess."

"If I had to pick a single number, ten's not a bad place to start. *Ten* times better off. But that's still just a number. Let me try to give you the flavor of what that change means. In 1900, only 15 percent of American households had flush toilets. Maybe 25 percent had running water. Housewives—and most women were housewives—washed clothes using a scrub board with water hauled from a well or a stream or a tenement faucet. That meant carrying about 10,000 gallons a year. About twelve hours every day were devoted to household chores. Half of that was food prep. Sound fun? A quarter of all households shared their living quarters with a lodger. No central heating. No refrigerators. Virtually no one had electricity. Maybe a fifth of all households had an icebox and access to ice. No microwaves. No cell phones. Forty percent of the American work force worked on the farm and worked seventy-four hours each week. City workers worked sixty hours a week. Our standard of living in America today dwarfs our standard of living of one hundred years ago by an enormous amount."

"I don't know if my generation is into money the way yours is."

"America's success since 1900 isn't really about money. It's about using that indoor toilet and having penicillin so you don't die from an infection. It's about women not dying in childbirth. In 1900, the chance of a woman in America dying during childbirth was about eight out of a thousand, almost 1 percent. Today, it's about eight out of 100,000. So childbirth is *one hundred times* safer than it was 100 years ago. Think that's about money? Or infant mortality. In 1900, one out of every ten—ten!—babies died in the first year of life. Today the mortality rate is under one out of one hundred. That's a *ten*fold improvement. It's about ridding the world of polio. It's about a shorter workweek or a longer retirement that leaves more time to spend with your family, or learning to paint or play the guitar. It's about painkillers. Try getting a tooth pulled in 1900 if you want to have some fun. There were about 6,000 books published in 1900. Today, about 300,000 books are published in a year. And it's about electric guitars and iPhones, too, the Internet and microwave ovens and everything else. Antibiotics and pacemakers. Skateboards and flavored dental floss. Artificial hearts and graphite tennis rackets. There are a lot of glorious and sublime things we have that we didn't have a hundred years ago and a lot of petty and trivial things, too. Our wealth makes it all possible."

"So do you think people are any happier now that they have all that money?" Ramon asked. "Do you think people with all those toys and even those flush toilets are happier than people back in 1900? People who had to use outhouses didn't spend a lot of time longing for a toilet. They got used to what they had. And maybe their lives had a lot more meaning. You said more of them worked on farms. They saw their crops come up. They were closer to the earth and the real source of things. Instead of shopping at a grocery store for food that is pumped full of chemicals and pesticides, they lived life for real. And you talk about quality? A lot of things were better back then. Food was better, for sure. Healthier. Just think about all that homemade bread in those farm houses."

"But I bet the coffee was a lot worse. Can you imagine a more deprived life than life without Starbucks?"

"Starbucks! They're—"

"It's a joke, Ramon. Relax. And although it's nice to grow your own food, when their crops didn't come up, it took some of the fun out of being close to the earth. But you make a good point. I don't think money makes you happy. I think poor people in 1900 could be just as joyous as rich people in 2000. But that having been said, I don't think people living today would like to travel back in time to be poor. And I'd guess that the average person—even a rich person—in 1900 sure would like to be alive in 2000 instead, even as distant from the land and artificial as our life might seem at times."

"Even if you're right, the poor person in 1900 transported to the richer world of today would soon find that the promise of all that wealth was an illusion. He or she would have the same troubles, the same stress, the same frustrations."

"Maybe, but people want to better themselves. They want more of everything. More toys, yes. More cars, more refrigerators, more iPhones. And more love. And more justice. And cleaner air. And more safety. Part of that urge is an illusion, just as you say. When you get more, you don't feel satisfied. After you win your first Wimbledon, you'll know all about it. You want it so badly, surely getting it will satisfy that part of you inside that cries out for success. Wimbledon! The top! Yet after awhile, you'll be just as hungry, just as unfulfilled as you are now. But that urge for more, that hunger—it leads to greatness. It leads to courage and sacrifice and persistence in the face of disappointment and defeat. It's a huge part of what makes us human."

"But the system caters to that urge in all kinds of unhealthy ways. The system stokes that urge with social pressure and advertising and promises that don't come true. Wouldn't it be a better world if there were less of a chance to satisfy that urge? If that urge wasn't free to run amok? Sure, income would be lower. But maybe we'd spend more time talking and laughing and less time working. And incomes would be more equal. The gap between rich and poor would be smaller. We'd get along better. Be closer to our neighbors."

"I like laughing and talking, too. What do you think I'm doing here on this bench?" Ramon laughed as Ruth continued. "Only a fool spends his time trying to make as much money as possible. As the saying goes—no one on his deathbed wishes he spent more time at the office. But I think the gap between rich and poor isn't as important as the gap between the poor today and the poor yesterday."

"What do you mean?"

"Take a dinner here at Stanford where a wealthy donor is being served by a waiter making a little more than the minimum wage. The donor may have his own jet, but even a waiter has usually flown on a jet at some time in his life, albeit in a coach seat. The donor may have been chauffeured to the dinner in a luxury car, but the waiter's Honda Civic is pretty quiet and comfortable. The rich guy wears a custom-made suit that may have cost over $1,000. But the waiter can afford a suit that's 100 percent wool and looks pretty good. Yes, the donor's watch is more expensive. But the waiter's digital model probably keeps better time. Unless the waiter stops by the donor's house for a visit, he's unlikely to feel the pinch of his lower income status the way he would have in 1900, when rich people rode in carriages and poor people walked. Rich people then had nice clothes and poor people dressed in cruder clothing made of coarser fabric. Rich people ate plenty and poor people often went hungry. Rich people had servants while poor people used washboards to keep their meager wardrobe clean and spent hours each day making meals. Today, almost half of all poor people own their own homes. Over half have cars or trucks to drive. They wear clothes made of soft cotton and wool and they have servants."

"Servants! What are you talking about, Professor Lieber?"

"Call me Ruth. Today, almost two-thirds of the poor families in America have washing machines. Over half have dryers. A third have a dishwasher. Those machines are servants, aren't they? And they're usually more reliable than the old-fashioned kind. Three-quarters of all poor households have air conditioning. In 1970, fewer than half of all households in America had air conditioning. Yes, the highest earning people today are making more than the highest earning people ten or twenty years ago or fifty or a hundred years ago. But so is everyone else. If your standard of living doubles but so does everyone else's, inequality is unchanged but surely you're better off. I think most people care about getting ahead, not about whether they're getting ahead of others. And for their children to be better off than they were. By that standard, America is still the land of opportunity. Look at your roots. Look at Cuba."

"Cuba's not as rich as America," Ramon said. "I'll grant you that. But it's a fairer society. There aren't people like Bill Gates or a bunch of Wall Street types living off everyone else."

"I don't think those people live off of others. And while there's no Bill Gates, you do get Castro—he's worth a few bucks, I'd guess. And I bet the folks in his circle of close friends are doing pretty well, too."

"But health care is free. Education is free. I think the literacy rate is higher there than here."

"And Castro's defenders think that makes up for living under tyranny."

"I won't defend the tyranny. I've heard too many stories from too many relatives. But you evidently think Americans are happier than Cubans."

"Actually, I have no idea how happy Cubans are. Or Americans, for that matter. It's a big country. But I know one thing and maybe it's the only thing to know."

"Yes?"

"Traffic only flows in one direction. To America. Nobody's swimming south trying to get into the worker's paradise.

Isn't that puzzling? We hear all the time about how horribly America treats its poor. But poor people in Mexico and Cuba risk death to be poor here. Death! That's because they know that if they are poor in Mexico or Cuba, the odds are good they'll be poor all their life. And their kids will be poor, too. But being poor here in America doesn't have to be a life sentence. People come to America poor. Their children lead better lives."

"You sound like my mother. Castro is evil and everything in America is perfect."

"Your mother makes my case. She came here with nothing. Her son will have everything, if he chooses. Was your mother deluded in thinking her life would be better here in America? I agree with you—it's not the Garden of Eden. But don't you think she finds more contentment here than she would have had she stayed in Cuba?"

"But in Cuba, my mother's neighborhood was a nice place to live. You should hear her talk about her friends and the ease of life. The kids running free, playing till all hours, safe. Not like here. Sure there weren't a lot of nice cars or fancy food. But people were close and no one felt like they were losing some economic race with the people on the other side of town. Miami's different. She's got no pride. She worries about crime. She's a cleaning lady, for God's sake!"

"I know. It looks like a dead end. But you're the way out of the cul-de-sac for her. And while I expect great things of you, Ramon, in many ways, you are no different from other immigrants born of immigrant parents. You will have an easier life than your mother."

"That's great. No pressure, but it's up to me to make my mother's life meaningful. Thanks a million."

"Relax. You've already taken care of her. You're going to graduate from Stanford. Stanford! What, do you feel guilty? Think it's your fault your mom isn't still in that nice neighborhood back in Havana?"

Ramon said nothing.

"It was her choice!" Ruth continued. "She made the call. She rolled the dice. Same with my mother. She came to New York City from Poland without a penny in her pocket. Worked as a seamstress. Horrible, tedious job. Sure, she'd tell me romantic stories about the old country. But like your mother, I think she edited out the bad scenes. And not everything she found here was as advertised. There were plenty of tough times. But my mother and your mother came here and put up with those tough times because they had their eye on a different prize and on different dreams, dreams for me and you. And some of those dreams came true."

"The land of dreams? It turned out OK for you and me. But for too many people it's a nightmare. Sometimes I think we're all just trapped in a game called 'whoever-has-the-most-toys wins.'"

"I accept part of your argument. Money isn't everything. But who's trapped? You told me five minutes ago that you're not going to worship money like my generation does. I think you misunderstand my generation. But if you're right, more power to you. You're free to live like a king. Better than any real-life king of history. And you're free to give it all away and live like a monk. The difference between America and Cuba is that in America, you're free to choose. In Cuba, you have to live like a monk. Besides, it's really hard to be happy when you're dead."

"Can't argue with that," Ramon said. "What do you mean?"

"That dying in childbirth thing. Way down over the last one hundred years. The odds of dying on the job have plummeted, too, in the last one hundred years. Life expectancy generally—way up. And I think we've just scratched the surface. You'll probably be able to live to well over a hundred. You might even have a chance to live to two hundred. And I don't mean a life where the last 110 years are spent sitting in a chair, a vacant look on your face because you can't remember anything. Quality of life for the elderly gets better all the time. We're going to get better and better at that. That's true wealth."

"OK, you're breaking me down. Even I like living longer. And I even admit to liking my iPhone."

"So how did it happen?" Ruth asked. "How did we get here from there? How did our lives change so much?"

When Ramon didn't answer, Ruth continued. "Don't you think it's strange that in America, the country where the greatest economic revolution in history has taken place, the average citizen has no idea why we're richer? If you had a goose that laid golden eggs, wouldn't you want to understand a little about its health? I mean, it's one thing to live in the Sinai desert and depend on the Almighty for sustenance. Maybe you wouldn't need to be curious about how fresh manna shows up every morning. But if we want to preserve what we have and continue this incredible run of economic success, shouldn't our citizens have some knowledge of how the thing works?"

Ramon started to wonder if he had misread Ruth Lieber's interest in talking to him. He had presumed she simply wanted to keep her hand in. Keep on his good side after she had admitted to him that she had been devious in warning him away from Heavy Weather. But maybe she was like that guy at the beach throwing the beached starfish back into the ocean. Someone comes along and says he's wasting his time, there are so many beached starfish, how can he hope to make a difference? Made a difference to that one, he says, throwing another one back. Maybe he was just a starfish to her. One more person she could educate about economics. Seemed pretty futile. Why should she bother? Maybe it was an obsession. Amy said she was pretty passionate about teaching.

"So what's the answer?" Ramon asked. "How did we get here from there?"

"Let's take a simple piece of the puzzle," Ruth answered. A school teacher in 1900 needed to work an hour to earn a dozen eggs. Today, a school teacher has to work about three minutes. A twentyfold drop in the price of eggs. How did it come to pass that teachers only have to work three minutes to earn a dozen eggs when they used to have to work an hour?"

"Are you telling me that life is better for school teachers because eggs are cheaper?"

"When we say that the standard of living of the average person is ten or twenty times higher today than it was in 1900, we're saying that the average person can buy ten or twenty times more of everything. The change in the affordability of eggs is just an example of something that's typical of most products and some services. People don't have to work nearly as long as they once did to afford to buy things."

"So why did you pick an egg as your example?"

"An egg today is a lot like an egg in 1900. It might have fewer blood spots. Maybe a bigger yolk. But it's not like the changes in portable music players. Eggs today are pretty similar to the eggs of yesterday. And the technology of teaching hasn't changed much either. So how come teachers can enjoy cheaper eggs?"

"Don't teachers make more money than they did in 1900?"

"They do. And eggs are more expensive. But the increase in salaries has been sufficiently large to lower the real price of eggs by a factor of 20. A teacher today has a higher standard of living. How did that happen?"

"They were probably exploited back in 1900, but now they have unions."

"Unions might have something to do with it, but unions can't be a very important explanation for why the real standard of living has risen dramatically for most if not all occupations over the last one hundred years. Over the last fifty years, salaries have risen dramatically at a time when unions have become increasingly unimportant. Yet salaries keep on rising. And in the nineteenth century, when there were no unions, the standard of living for the average American rose steadily, too. Something else must be going on."

"But what keeps workers from being exploited without unions?"

"Workers have choices. There are lots of different places to work. If you want to attract good employees, you have to treat them well. Look at your mom. What do you think she earns cleaning houses?"

"Not enough. Do you know how much tennis lessons cost? It's grotesque. Do you know how many toilets she had to clean so I could have one hour of a tennis pro's time? That's my measure of purchasing power. And just like yours, it doesn't correct for quality. My mom's hours are spent scrubbing the floor or a toilet, while the tennis pro gets to swing the racket and talk. He doesn't even bend over to pick up the loose tennis balls! They've got someone who does that. There's something wrong with this picture."

"I'm sure she deserves better. But how do we get there from here? I don't know a way to make housecleaning pay better that doesn't hurt the people you're trying to help."

"What do you mean by that?"

"If you passed a special minimum wage for maids on the grounds that their jobs deserve more, you'd discourage people from hiring them. The best ones might still get hired. But some people would stop using a housecleaner if it got too expensive. I don't think that's a very thoughtful way to help—"

"Forget about the minimum wage. The whole system is flawed. There's no justice."

"Hang on. If you think housecleaners are exploited, why aren't they exploited even more? People who clean houses make anything between $10 and $20 an hour, depending on the city. Why would people pay even $10 an hour to have someone clean their house? That's almost more than twice the minimum wage. And in big cities, people pay three or four times the minimum wage. There's no union. It's an unregulated cash business. Why don't people pay less?"

"Guilt?"

"Always a possibility. But that's a lot of people with quite a conscience. I have a different explanation. People pay their housecleaners more than the minimum wage because they have to."

"I thought you said it was unregulated," Ramon said.

"Sorry. Bad choice of words. I meant that if you want someone to clean your house, you have to pay more than the minimum wage or no one will show up. The maids have alternatives. They're not trapped. Oh, they're not as free as a Stanford undergraduate, that's true. But they're not at the mercy of the upper classes either. Back in 1900, a maid earned maybe $240 a year and worked twelve hours a day, six days a week. That's about seven cents an hour. A dozen eggs in 1900 cost twenty cents. So it took a maid in 1900 about three hours of work to earn a dozen eggs. Today, a maid who earns $10 an hour has to pay about $1 for a dozen eggs. Six minutes! So eggs are thirty times cheaper for someone who cleans houses today compared to someone who cleaned houses a hundred years ago. How did that happen? It can't be unions. The housekeeper today doesn't have a union and neither did the one back then. The technology of housecleaning—or teaching for that matter—hasn't changed much. In the case of housecleaning, you take some rags and brooms and soap and clean. The vacuum cleaner helps, but cleaning a house is still mainly a lot of physical labor. In the case of teaching, a teacher stands up in front of a class and talks, walks around, uses paper and books."

"So the change is something that happened in the egg business."

"Seems like it. But how could the egg business change? Look at the technology of egg-laying. It hasn't changed since the dawn of creation. It's all inside the chicken. How can you improve it? You feed the chicken. It lays an egg. You pick up the egg. You sell it."

"You can breed better chickens. You could study what chicken feed works best. There must be ways of improving productivity."

"Sure. But the biggest changes were figuring out ways to make the workers more productive."

"The workers?"

"Yes. Chickens lay eggs. But people get those eggs from the egg farm to your refrigerator. People take care of the chickens, people collect the eggs, people put the eggs into containers. Look at the job of taking care of the chickens and collecting the eggs—the job of running the hen house. Two people can oversee 800,000 chickens that produce 240 million eggs a year. *Two hundred forty million!* Can you imagine it? The average worker produces 120 million eggs in a year."

"It must be a big chicken coop."

"It is. But imagine me giving you the following assignment. I'll be back in a year. Please deliver 240 million eggs to me over the next year. I'll give you the chickens and the feed and even some medical supplies to keep the chickens healthy. You can use a friend to help. The two of you need to find a way to get 240 million eggs produced over the year. It won't be too hard. All you have to do is keep track of 3 million chickens."

"Wait a minute. You said you only need 800,000 chickens."

"Those are healthy, caged American chickens with perfectly calibrated diets, water, heat, and everything else. But I'm not letting you use modern technology. You're going to have to raise them the way they were raised in 1900, roughly the way chickens are raised today in the Third World. So you're going to need four times as many chickens. I'll give you a big field, a big scratching yard for your chickens to wander in. A very big field. You and your buddy are standing in this field, looking out at the expectant faces of your 3 million new clucking friends. Chickens as far as the eye can see. They're hungry and thirsty. And they fight with each other. The noise alone would be something. Let me give you one more idea of the challenge you're going to face. To meet the quota of 240 million eggs per year, all you need to do is collect about 650,000 eggs each day. Seems like a big number, doesn't it?"

"Yes, it does."

"It *is* a big number. Even if you could pick up four eggs every *second*, two in each hand, which won't be easy because you're going to have to put the eggs in some kind of container and whatever kind of container you're going to use, it's going to get filled up and that's going to bite into your four-eggs-a-second pace, but even if you could keep up that pace somehow, it's going to take you forty-six hours a day to pick up those 650,000 eggs. *Forty-six hours.* But that's OK. You've got a partner. So you can divide the egg-collecting duties in half. That's only twenty-three hours a day each. That leaves you a whole hour every day to eat, sleep, and balance your checkbook. Oh, and you'll also have to squeeze in feeding the chickens, keeping them disease-free, and moving out the ones that die."

"I see it's going to be a little bit of a challenge. So how can two people get it done today?"

In the past, even a hundred years ago, a farmer let his chickens run around. Then he'd go in the yard and see if any eggs were out there. Someone had the idea of having a hen house, so you could at least limit the number of places to look for eggs. Then they put the chickens in cages so it would be even easier to find the eggs and the chickens would be less likely to kill themselves fighting or give each other diseases. Then they put the coops underground to keep them cooler. Built them on an angle to use gravity to deliver food and water. Mechanized the whole thing to reduce labor costs and improve the reliability of the feeding and the ventilation, used fluorescent light and better and more feed to increase egg-laying rates. Scraped off the chicken droppings to use for fertilizer. They even tried fitting the chickens with contact lenses."

"You're kidding."

"No, red light seems to help chickens lay eggs. So they were trying red contact lenses—rose-colored glasses for chickens. Incredible, isn't it?"

"It's amazing. The whole thing sounds pretty tough on the chickens. I read somewhere that they cut off their beaks. So here are these de-beaked chickens living in cages. They're egg-laying prisoners."

"It's probably not a pretty sight. Does it bother you?"

"Yes, it does."

"The marketplace actually caters to your discomfort. You can buy eggs from free-range chickens if you're willing to pay a premium. Then again, you might not want to romanticize the life of a chicken. When some people think of a free-range chicken, they think of something like Julie Andrews in *The Sound of Music* whirling across a meadow warbling. They see a chicken unshackled, bounding across a farmyard. But true free-range chickens spend the night worrying about coyotes and die from infections passed on by ticks. And then there are the human consequences. In the Third World, a typical chicken might lay eighty eggs a year. A little over one a week. An American chicken can lay over three hundred, almost one a day. If you were starving to death or your kid was, I'd think you'd like to have one of those productive, oppressed American prisoner chickens that lays an egg almost every day rather than one of those fulfilled, high self-esteem Third World chickens that lays only once a week, scratching around in a poor person's backyard."

"Fair enough."

"So here's the puzzle. What created all that knowledge of how to produce eggs more cheaply? Why did farmers try to find ways to get eggs more efficiently?"

"Seems pretty simple," Ramon answered. "If you can lower your costs, you make more profit. I remember that from my economics class."

"And therein lies one of the great fallacies."

"What do you mean? You don't make higher profits when your costs go down?"

"Here's the fallacy. If you can remember this, you have a chance of being a pretty fair economist. What's the definition of profits?"

"Revenue minus costs."

"Right. So if costs go down, profits should go up. If you subtract a smaller number from revenues, profits are higher."

"Look. I'm no math whiz. But I can handle this. What's the trick?"

"You're making an implicit assumption when you conclude that profits are going up. You're making an implicit assumption that revenues are constant."

"Oh, sure. So? When you cut costs, you make higher profits. I still think this is right. Am I missing something?"

"Yes. You're missing the relation between costs and revenue. There are two connections. One is obvious. The other is hidden. There are two ways to cut costs. One is to cut corners and lower the quality of your product. Use inferior materials, make the product with less quality oversight, reduce the number of bells and whistles on the product that cost money. You've made your product crummier. You'll have to lower your price and you're likely to sell fewer units. So cutting costs lowers revenues. Whether profits go up or down depends on whether the savings in costs are large enough to outweigh the loss in revenues. You can go out of business if you try to cut costs this way."

"But that's not the kind of cost cutting we're talking about," Ramon said. "We're talking about innovations that lower the costs of production for the farmer but keep the quality of the egg unchanged for the consumer. That has to increase profits."

"For the first farmer that innovates or the first few, yes. They'll do better. They might even do a lot better for a while. But as those innovations get copied by the other farmers, the price of eggs is going to fall and so are the profits. It's only a matter of time before too many eggs are chasing too few egg eaters. And when that happens, price falls."

"Why are there going to be too many eggs on the market?"

"Because those initial profits are going to inspire a bunch of new people to start up egg farms to get at those riches."

"But how are people going to know? Right now, egg farming could be the most profitable occupation in the world. How would I know? I don't read the *Egg Farmers Gazette* that has all those pictures of egg farmers driving Lexuses and BMWs. That's one thing I never understood about economics. My professor would say that profits encourage people to do this or that. But that assumes everyone's paying attention. Most people aren't paying attention."

"Not everyone has to pay attention. Even if no one is paying attention, the price of eggs is going to fall because there's going to be an increase in the supply of eggs."

"How's that?"

"Every farmer who's already in the egg business is going to be making more money than before. Some of them, maybe all of them, are going to expand. They're going to want to add chickens to their flocks. To make even more money. When they expand, there will be more eggs on the market than there were before and the price will fall."

"But won't they kill the goose that lays the golden egg? If they all expand and the price of eggs goes down, the farmers aren't going to make the money they thought they were going to make. They should just be content with what they have and not expand."

"Nice idea. Unfortunately for egg farmers and fortunately for egg eaters, it's almost impossible to keep everyone from expanding. There's always the fear that some other farmers are going to expand while you stand pat. Then price falls and instead of being content with what you have, you're going to have to be content with a lot less. So you expand, too. Even if every farmer could agree not to expand, and if every farmer could know with certainty that everyone was keeping their promise not to expand, there are all the nonfarmers out there who are going to want in on the action."

"But I asked you before, how do they find out about this incredible opportunity? The egg farmers aren't going to be waving it about. They want to keep it quiet."

"But there are too many people who know all about it. And they are precisely the people, not you and me, who are likely to do something with that knowledge. They are the people who work on the egg farms or work on businesses associated with egg farming. Take the contractors who build the new chicken coops that are sloped and underground to save costs on delivering the food and the water. They know all about the new way of getting eggs. And they want to spread the word about the innovations so they can get more business."

"I don't know. I think businesses are pretty good at finding ways to make money."

"Sure they are. But look at the last one hundred years. There's been a revolution in how eggs get to your table. Farmers used their ingenuity to find new and cheaper ways to get eggs produced. Some of those insights came from government-funded research—it wasn't just the drive of farmers. But the interesting thing is who got almost all of the benefits from those insights and productivity improvements. Not the farmers! We did! The egg eaters. The price of eggs fell by a factor of 20 or 30. The egg farmers didn't want to pass on those cost savings in the form of lower prices. They wanted to keep them for themselves, just like anyone would. But the market didn't let them keep those savings. Competition between the farmers forced the prices down and forced the farmers to give most of the benefits to us. Now I can finally tell you how I can sleep at night letting companies like Big Box make all those profits. You learned about supply and demand in that economics course, right?"

"Yes."

"Can you draw it?" Ruth asked.

"It may have been a few semesters back, but I did learn something."

"Here." She handed him a notepad and a pen from her purse. Ramon quickly sketched a supply curve and a demand curve crossing it.

"Excellent. That's how every economist draws it too. What letter does it look like?"

"An X."

"That's right. Two diagonal lines sloping in opposite directions, crossing in the middle. Now tell me this. According to economics, who has the upper hand? The suppliers or the demanders? The sellers or the buyers?"

"Neither, under what was it called, perfect competition?"

"That's right. Under perfect competition, the benefits of transacting, the so-called 'gains from trade,' are shared by both buyers and sellers. Buyers pay less than the maximum price they'd be willing to pay. Sellers receive more than the minimum they need to stay in business. And what protects each side from the greed of the other? What economists call competition. There are lots of sellers in the supply and demand picture. And lots of buyers. So no one has too much power. Now suppose we went over to the mall or to a movie theater or a popular restaurant or a public park, and asked normal human beings—noneconomists—the same question—: who has the upper hand, buyers or sellers? What do you think they'd say?"

"The sellers."

"I agree. That is what most people think. So what gives? Economists claim the power of sellers is restrained by competition. Everyday Americans think sellers have the upper hand. Who's right?"

"They could both be right. Perfect competition is just a theory, isn't it? So it's the wrong theory."

"Could be. So tell me this. If the sellers have the upper hand in the real world, and if economic theory says that the power is shared evenly, then how does it turn out that eggs cost consumers one-twentieth or one-thirtieth of what they did one hundred years ago? A hundred years ago, eggs were expensive for poor people. If you'd been alive back then, you might have wanted to do something about that. It would have been easy to make eggs cheaper. But it's a lot harder to make cheaper eggs."

"Now I'm totally confused."

"We could have passed legislation one hundred years ago mandating low prices for eggs, a price ceiling. But that wouldn't have truly made eggs cheaper. That wouldn't have changed how many people it took to produce one hundred eggs. In fact, by taking the profit out of egg making, a price ceiling on eggs would have discouraged people from producing eggs. So eggs would be cheap, but very few people would be able to buy them. Somehow, we got cheaper eggs without mandating lower prices. And not just eggs. Over the last one hundred years, producers have found ways to lower the cost of producing virtually everything. And the savings were passed on to the consumer in the form of lower prices rather than being kept by the suppliers in the form of higher profits. How can that be? Why is the average American—the average American, not the richest American—why is the average American maybe *ten times* better off than a hundred years ago? And it might be as high as *twenty or thirty times* better off. How did those greedy business owners and corporate moguls let that happen?"

"I give up."

"Did the owners of companies and big-shot CEOs decide in a gesture of kindness to allow consumers a break?"

"I doubt it."

"Did they lose their competitive edge and go soft?"

"I doubt that too. So why did they do it?"

"All of those businesses and CEOs over the last one hundred years would have liked bigger profits. But competition drove them to give them away. They weren't in charge of deciding who gets what. Each CEO is in charge of his or her own company. But no one's in charge of the whole system. It means that prices depend on the actions of individuals trying to do the best they can for themselves. Ironically, perhaps, that means consumers triumph, even in a world of greedy business owners."

"So the man or woman on the street is wrong and the economists are right?"

"No, the economists are wrong, too, if by the economists, you mean supply and demand as a way of capturing what's going on over time. Without some creative finagling, it does a lousy job of capturing the real competition that underlies every moment and every corner of the American economy. The picture misses the ceaseless striving for excellence that the market demands of sellers, driving them to lower costs. Followed by lower prices. Followed by a higher standard of living."

"You're saying people figure stuff out and it makes all of us richer."

"There's more to it than that." Ruth looked at her watch. "But I've got a meeting. Sorry. Maybe we'll talk some more another time."

"See you tonight, then."

"Tonight?"

"Aren't you having your students over for dinner? Amy invited me to come with her. That's OK, isn't it?"

"Absolutely," she said. She had told the students they could bring a friend. "But you belong there, anyway. You're one of my students now."

She winked and walked away.

8

A NIGHT IN THE CEMETERY

There are rumors about Castro's health flying around the capital and the countryside like flies around raw meat. This is an old sport in the capital and everyone gets to play. But this time, some of the rumors are true. A myriad of crises are happening at the same time, each one making things difficult for the heart. There is cancer and chemotherapy. An infection has settled in the lungs and there are drugs working to reverse it. The kidneys are tired and want to stop working altogether.

In the face of these failures, is there really any hope of recovery? The Leader's body is like a car on an icy road where each skid toward the ditch threatens to be answered by the yanking of the steering wheel that may send the car into the traffic from the on-coming lane. Each doctor has a hand on the wheel and while each wishes to stay on the road, it is late and getting darker and darker. Barring a miracle or a curse, it is only a matter of time.

Ruth Lieber lived on one of those quiet Palo Alto streets to the south of the Stanford campus east of El Camino. Not a big house and not a small one—a house that in a medium-sized American city in the Midwest or the South would be worth maybe $250,000 but in Palo Alto was worth a great deal more.

Every year, at the end of her senior seminar, Ruth invited the students over to her house for dinner. White wooden chairs were spread around the backyard. A long table held platters of grilled chicken, potato salad, cole slaw, and spinach salad. There were grilled vegetables and tofu for the vegetarians. On a smaller table was an enormous cooler filled with soda and bottled water.

Ruth Lieber moved among her students and their guests, making everyone comfortable and making sure everyone had enough to eat and drink. She made a particular effort to draw out the friends who accompanied her students.

Night fell on the garden and the crowd thinned out. The voices got quieter and soon only Ramon and Amy and a handful of others were still there. Ramon looked at his watch and saw it was well past nine o'clock.

"Time to go," he announced. "Let's help clean up."

"Forget it," Ruth protested.

Ramon ignored her and began gathering up the folding chairs scattered around the lawn. Amy began carrying the leftovers into the kitchen. The others quickly pitched in and in a few minutes all the garbage and food was cleared away.

The remaining guests hugged Ruth one last time and extracted promises from her to meet their parents at graduation. Soon, only Ramon and Amy were left. Standing by the door, ready to leave, Ramon saw a room off the living room with a single light burning over a desk. He wandered over to the doorway. There was a heavy oak desk against one wall. A large leather armchair in a corner.

"Kenny's study. My husband. He died four years ago." Ruth was at Ramon's side and Amy had followed. "It's not a shrine. I've cleaned most of the stuff out. But I left the furniture as is. And I like leaving his light on."

The wall across from the desk was covered with photos of Ruth, her husband, their children, and their grandchildren.

Ruth pointed out the pictures of her grandchildren from St. Louis and Amy told Ramon the story of the nervous father and the surprise side trip to the gas station. Then Amy glanced over at the desk, trying to figure out why it was covered with what looked like oversized dominos in neat rows.

"What are these?" she asked.

"Pick one up," Ruth said. "Check it out. When a company goes public, the underwriters usually run an ad in the *Wall Street Journal* or somewhere, telling the world that such-and-such a company has gone public and then it gives some of the details—the number of shares and so on."

"What's an underwriter?"

"An investment firm that helps a company go public—it writes the prospectus, sells it to the brokerage houses who in turn sell it to the investing public. Kenny helped with every one of those. Those were companies he had nurtured and worked with. So when they went public they sent him a souvenir—a miniature copy of the ad embedded in lucite. It's a common practice. He called his desktop the cemetery."

Amy looked puzzled.

"When he was alive," Ruth continued, "it was a lot messier than this. It was where papers and books and memos went to die until they were sometimes resurrected in a flurry of cleaning activity. But the other reason is that those ads are called 'tombstones.' That's why he liked to line them up in those neat little rows. But you have to understand that calling it the cemetery was really ironic. They shouldn't call them tombstones. They should call them birth announcements—when a company goes public, that's when you know the dream is really alive."

"So he should have called it the maternity ward, not the cemetery," Amy suggested.

"Kenny would have liked that idea," Ruth said, smiling. "That's very sweet. His company really was an incubator of sorts. He liked having these on his desk to remind himself of why he put up with all the paperwork and the crazy hours and all the twists and turns of starting a company. You do that all day and you can forget why you're doing it in the first place."

Ramon started to say something but stopped. Ruth knew what he was thinking. It's all for the money, isn't it? Ruth could see it written on his face.

"Amy, can you hand me one of those tombstones?"

"Any one in particular?"

"No, just take one. It doesn't matter."

They all looked the same to Amy, anyway. Blocks of lucite, about the size of a deck of cards. Encased in each one was a page out of a newspaper, shrunk down, lots of little print. Amy took one at random and handed it to Ruth. She smiled.

"A good one?" Amy asked.

"Yes. Every one of those blocks has a story behind it. But you picked a good one."

Ruth took the desk chair and turned it around. Ramon and Amy took the leather-upholstered footstool from in front of the armchair in the corner and slid it toward Ruth. Then they sat down facing her.

"Warson Industries," Ruth said, holding the lucite block toward Ramon and Amy. "Tom Warson was like a lot of people my husband worked with—an engineer who liked making things. And like many of them, he paid a steep price to go off on his own. Sure, it's nice to be your own boss and to have the chance to make what is sometimes a very large

amount of money. But in return, you take on an incredible amount of risk. And tension. Most of the people behind
those tombstones put all they had into those companies. And
I mean all they had. All the money. All the time. All the imagination. All the passion. There's not much left over for your
spouse or the kids if you have a family. Or yourself."

"Like you told me the other day," Ramon said. No one
on his deathbed wishes he'd spent more time at the office."

"That's right."

"Doesn't that cast a different light on these tombstones?
Here are a bunch of men and women who gave it all. For
what? For money? For going public?"

"But Ramon. You told me that you don't play tennis for
the money."

"I don't!"

"I believe you. So you of all people know that money and
passion going together doesn't mean the passion comes from
the money."

"But there's passion and there's obsession. You make it
sound like the people who started these companies went over
the edge. A lot of them anyway." He couldn't help thinking
there was something wrong with someone who devoted his
life to a company instead of his friends and family.

"I know it looks like some kind of macabre scoreboard,"
Ruth said. "But there's more to the story. See this one?" Ruth
asked, picking up one of the lucite dominoes off the desk.
"This company developed a whole new line of bike helmets
that were so hip, kids actually *wanted* to wear them. They had
some tough times raising money for a bike helmet company when everyone else was creating the latest dot-com that
promised to change the world. The woman who started it

had a terrible time keeping the rest of her life together while she built her company. But at least she could remind herself that she was helping kids protect themselves. That you can at least imagine as something worth sacrificing for."

"Sure," Ramon agreed. "But what about Tom Warson?"

"That's why I'm glad you picked Warson Industries. Warson Industries didn't help make kids safer or cure AIDS with some new gene therapy. There was no romance about Tom's company. All it did was make some piece of hardware that was used in routers or servers. I don't remember the technical name. Something to do with the backbone of the Internet. Hardware with a small 'h.' Not even a new disk drive or some geek gadget that fits in your pocket, keeps your schedule, and brews perfect coffee at the same time. More like something you'd find in Home Depot if computer companies shopped there. Can you think of a less romantic product? Sometimes I'd tease Tom that his company name should really have been Widget Industries. A widget is the word economists use when we don't want to think of a real example. It's just a silly name for 'thing.' That's how bland his product was."

"But there are a lot of vertebrae in the backbone of the Internet. I'd guess he did OK," Ramon said.

"He did. But even when you have a home run like Tom's idea, there are still plenty of ups and downs. He had a bunch of designs that failed. And then when he finally succeeded on the design end, there were still plenty of adventures. You think you're going to win a big contract that's going to help you make your numbers, but you miss a deadline for a proposal because you're short on staff, trying to nurse your capital. The parts you need don't get to you in time because you're brand new and your credit rating isn't so hot. There's some permit you need that you didn't know about, so your factory doesn't open when it's supposed to. A hundred things go wrong. A thousand things. And remember the stakes. Every setback slows you down physically and emotionally. And you can't show any of that anxiety to the world. Otherwise, your employees might look for other jobs, your investors might not give you that next round of funding. Everything has to be 100 percent fine and getting even better. You can't ever let them see you sweat."

"Sounds like a nightmare. I guess the chance to get rich keeps some people going," Amy said.

"The money matters. You might get a kick out of rolling the dice when there's $10 on the table. But it's a lot more fun with your life savings and your marriage and your reputation on the line. Fun's the wrong word. Maybe—"

"Exhilarating?" Amy suggested. "The ultimate cure for a mid-life crisis? Like my dad when he bought a BMW convertible."

"That's right. The money keeps the adrenaline pumping. And look at it this way. If you're going to put your life on the line and your future, wouldn't you rather make more money than less? But there's a lot more going on. A lot of these entrepreneurs would be over here to talk to Kenny about something, late at night, on some kind of deadline, and while Kenny finished up the phone call he was on, or the papers he had brought home from the office, I'd talk to them. I think they'd talk to me in a way they couldn't talk with anyone else, not their spouses, not their investors, not their friends. They knew I wouldn't judge them if they sounded weak or scared or—"

"Or human?" Ramon said.

"That's right. Or just human. Tom Warson must have been here a dozen times for this or that. And we'd talk. But the time I'll never forget was one of the good times. Tom came here for dinner the Sunday night when everything had finally fallen into place. Everything was copacetic. Everything was—"

"Copawhat?" Ramon asked.

"Copacetic. A-OK. Smooth sailing. The factory had finally opened. Three months later than planned, but it had opened. And widgets were rolling off the line and heading out to customers. Orders were being filled. Tom brought his wife—he was one of the lucky ones, his marriage survived the experience—and the four of us sat down at the table. We were all excited, as you'd expect, but Tom was beyond excitement. He couldn't stop talking about the factory and how many units they did in the first week and how many they'd do in the first month and the first year and the next and on and on. He was already talking about new products he'd add to the line, deluxe widgets, widgets with sensors, widgets that could think, widgets that could repair themselves. Finally his wife said, 'Tom. Maybe we should talk about something else?' She was smiling but there was some tension there. He grinned sheepishly and went quiet."

Ruth was lost in thought for a moment, remembering that night. Then she went on.

"At the end of the evening, after dinner and lots of champagne, Tom and I were alone at the table for a moment. His wife must have been in the bathroom and Kenny must have been getting dessert or doing something in the kitchen. Tom looked across the table at me and whispered, 'I've got something for you. Put out your hand.' I liked Tom. I liked him a lot. And I was very happy for him that night. But I almost couldn't get my arm out onto the table. There was such a conspiratorial intensity in his voice and in his eyes that I wouldn't have been surprised if he'd pressed some LSD into my palm. Somehow, I managed to reach across the table and he put something golden in my hand, closing his fingers over mine. You'd have thought it was the Holy Grail, or a gem of enormous value and he was asking me to leave my husband and run away with him. But of course, it wasn't a diamond."

"It was a widget," Amy said quietly.

"That's right. It was a widget."

"I guess he was pretty proud of it," Amy said.

"Sure. I don't blame him. I knew what that piece of metal had cost him. Money. Time. Energy. A big chunk of his life went into that chunk of metal. I knew he'd struggled with his marriage. Even his health had suffered. So I asked him—I asked him the question I always wanted to ask the ones who make it, who survive. Was it worth it?"

Ruth paused again, lost in memories.

"What did he say?" Ramon asked. It was so quiet in the little room he could hear the clock ticking. But Ruth could hear her husband fussing around in the kitchen.

"He said something I'll never forget. He didn't answer my question directly. Instead he said, 'When I saw the first one come off the line,' and then he stopped, looking for the words. 'All I could think about was my father. He died two years ago. I wish he could have been there. My father! And I didn't even like my father!' I just sat there. I couldn't think of anything to say. Then Kenny came back and the wife. The moment passed. But for the rest of the night, I couldn't stop thinking about Tom and his father, a man he 'didn't even like.' Why would he say something like that?"

"Maybe his father had told him once that he wouldn't amount to anything," Amy said. "And he wanted to prove him wrong. Maybe creating that company was Tom's way of slaying that dragon called fear of failure."

"Maybe," Ruth said. "But it can't have been the whole story. You should have heard the wistfulness in his voice when he mentioned his father. And the emotion he struggled to control."

"So what do you think?" Ramon asked.

"I think he realized what his father had put inside him. Even though he may not have liked him, Tom wanted his father to share in his success. And he wanted his father's approval. His respect. Probably his love. I think Tom saw his success as some crazy kind of redemption. His sense of self had been on the line, he had rolled the dice, and he had won. I think it was worth it in a way I'll never be able to understand. But I do know one thing. When all the hard work had paid off and that first widget came down the line, Tom Warson wasn't thinking of how rich he was going to get. I don't think the money had much to do with it at all."

Amy turned the lucite tablet over and over in her hand. Ramon sat quietly, lost in thought. Was he thinking of his own father, Ruth wondered, the man he had hardly known, but who must have passed on some kind of competitive fire, some urge to strive and excel? Was he imagining triumphs his father would never see?

"There it is," Ruth said, pointing to a chunk of burnished metal sitting on a bookshelf in a corner. She took it down and handed it to Amy. "The widget. No one on his deathbed wishes he'd spent more time at the office. But everyone on his deathbed regrets the dreams that got away. It's gold-plated, but when I see it, I only think of a man and his dreams."

Somewhere in the house, a clock chimed.

"Eleven o'clock," Ramon said. "We should go. Sorry we stayed so late."

"That's OK. I like to have a reason to sit in this room."

Ramon and Amy wandered into the night. Ruth went into the dining room, picked out a glass of finely etched crystal, and poured herself a shot of Lagavulin. She went back into the study and slid the big leather footstool back in front of the armchair. She leaned back in the armchair and put her feet up. When the glass was empty, Ruth Lieber turned off the light at her husband's desk and headed for dreamland.

9

THE PRICE OF EVERYTHING

The bleaker Castro's physical prospects, the more frantic are the doctors' efforts. Everyone is putting on a show. But they know it is only a matter of time. They cannot help it, but they are already thinking about the brave new world that is dawning, a world where everything might be different. A world where people who are friendly today will not be friendly tomorrow. A world where people who are dangerous today will be harmless tomorrow. A different world.

The next morning, when Ramon Fernandez finished running laps around the Stanford track, he was surprised to find Ruth Lieber leaning against the low fence surrounding the track, looking as if she were waiting for him. Was she waiting for him?

"Hello, Ruth. Thanks for dinner last night."

"My pleasure. You ought to marry that girl."

"Amy?" Ramon laughed. "Are you serious?"

"What's so crazy about it? She's a gem. Plus, I saw the way she looked at you. I saw the way you looked at her."

Ramon laughed again.

"Look, Ruth. Before I get I married I think I ought to figure out what I want to be when I grow up."

"You're pretty skilled with a tennis racket. I can personally vouch for the quality of your serve. And I hear very good things about the rest of your game."

"I may not be as good as I think I am. I may just burn out. I may blow out my knee. I'm just a promise waiting to be kept or broken."

"That's a nice line."

"It's my mom's. She likes to remind me so that I'll spend a little time in the classroom."

Ruth smiled.

"Besides," Ramon went on, "even if that promise is kept, it lasts for what—ten years? I'll need a life after tennis. What will that be?"

"I think you could do just about anything you want, tennis or no tennis. You don't have to figure out exactly what that will be right now."

"I know. But Amy's on a very different track. She's headed to grad school in biology. And she's thinking about med school. I'm a jock. Her dad's a senator, for heaven's sake. My mom's a cleaning lady."

"Take it back!"

Ramon saw anger in Ruth's eyes for the first time. She grabbed his shoulders. The strength in her hands surprised him. "Take it back! Your mother is not a cleaning lady! She's a wise woman who keeps your head on straight. Never confuse a person's identity or value as a human being with her job title. They have nothing to do with each other."

Ramon stood quietly, head down, accepting her rebuke.

"And your father?" Ruth continued. "I googled your father the other day. There was more life and pride and skill in your father than in a dozen senators!"

Ramon looked up.

"I hardly remember him," he said softly. "But I know what he was and what he meant to the people of Cuba."

"I'm sorry, Ramon. I was way out of line. I had no right to talk to you that way."

"No, you're right. I shouldn't have said that about my mom. I didn't mean it the way it sounded. Last summer, I stopped off at Amy's house." He stopped and shook his head in disbelief, remembering the grandeur of her parent's place in Georgetown. "It's just a little weird to think about—"

"What? Your mother visiting Amy's parents? Amy's parents coming to Miami?"

"Yeah."

Ruth left it alone. Ramon thanked Ruth again for dinner and headed into the tennis center to change and shower. Ruth took a seat on a bench just outside the front of the building. She looked at her watch. Five minutes until her meeting at ten. She tried to remember her schedule. A fifteen-minute consult with an alum raising money for the engineering school who needed her help getting the attention of a potential donor. Then a meeting with the dean of Arts and Sciences to strategize about the next step in securing the Big Box contribution. Then a lunch for a charity whose board she was on. There was something important later in the afternoon. She couldn't remember but it was much later. She leaned back and stretched. Pacific oaks wrapped her in shade. The hills were green in the distance. She closed her eyes for a moment. If she hurried, she could get back to her office in time to meet that alum. But she didn't get up. She reached for her purse and turned off her cell phone, took a deep breath and let her mind float off to the clouds above those green hills and waited. She probably wouldn't get fired. Probably.

"You're still here," Ramon said when he came back out, fifteen minutes later.

"It's a slow day," she lied. "I'm just enjoying the sun on my face and the fragrance of the air. It's a shame to take it all for granted. I try not to."

"Actually, I'm glad you're here. I wanted to ask you about something we talked about last night. Is it really a slow day? You probably—"

"No, I always have time for a few minutes of economics."

Ramon really wanted to ask her why she was stalking his workouts, googling his father, and spending so much time with him. Did she really have a slow schedule this close to graduation? His theory was that the whole thing, the seemingly chance meetings, the conversations, the attention, were all an attempt to get him to soften his graduation speech. It was vintage Ruth Lieber. Rather than trying to control things directly by banning him from the podium or threatening him with dire consequences, she would try to win him over with attention like their conversation last night.

"That story about that guy and the widgets—"

"Tom Warson?"

"Yeah. Tom Warson. It was a sweet story, but do you really believe that money had nothing to do with motivating him? Do you really believe people do things out of the goodness of their heart or their passion to impress their fathers? Aren't economists supposed to be big on incentives?"

"I didn't quite say that the money didn't matter. People tend to think about motivation as A or B, on or off, one thing or another. But that's not how people really behave. I'm a good example. I love my job. I love teaching. I love being part of making a university great. I love talking to students. I love my job. But if they didn't pay me, I'd stop showing up."

Ramon smiled.

"I stole that from another economist," Ruth admitted. "It captures how economists look at motivation. It's multifaceted. We care about money and we care about the other aspects of a job. Forget me. Look at you. I'd bet you'd make an incredible fly fisherman. Why don't you devote as much time to fly-fishing as you do to tennis? Here you are trying to be the greatest tennis player in the world when you could be the greatest fly fisherman!"

"That's silly. Ridiculous."

"But why?" Ruth countered. "It's silly because it doesn't matter if you're the best fly fisherman. But does it really matter if you're the best tennis player?"

"It matters to me."

"Why?"

"I love tennis. You can't imagine what it's like out there on center court, the game on the line, the crowd roaring with every ace."

"And if no one were watching? If there were no trophies? No crowd? Would it be as much fun?"

"I guess not."

"It would actually be like fly-fishing. Maybe a delightful experience, but not the same. I actually like fly-fishing. My father taught me how to cast when I was a girl. It's a wonderful experience. But I spent more time getting good at economics than I did at fly-fishing. And you're the same way. I'm sure there are things you enjoy that you spend time at that have no monetary payoff. Those things—reading poetry, listening to jazz, laughing with friends over a story at dinner—those are all glorious things. But it's also good to devote serious time to the things that pay."

"Sounds pretty mercenary."

"Money is one thing—I emphasize the word 'one'—one thing that motivates people. You might still decide to be a tennis player even if the prize money was a fraction of what it is now. I wouldn't tell you to take up golf, say, if golfers made more money than tennis players. I always tell my students on the last day of class not to choose their first job on the basis of money. But I don't tell them to take the job that pays the least. Without money and the motivation it provides, we'd have no idea how to serve our fellows."

"What are you talking about?" Ramon was totally bewildered by this absurd claim.

"Can I tell you a story?" Ruth asked.

"Can I stop you?" Ramon smiled.

"It's about another one of those entrepreneurs my husband worked with, David Kornfeld, an Israeli, a genius. He developed a laser that blasted the plaque from people's arteries without having to pry their chests open using open-heart surgery. It didn't work for everybody, but when it did, it was a miracle. The company experienced the typical challenges of any company that deals with medical devices. They lost their funding and David almost lost control of the company. FDA approval took forever. Some initial results that looked incredibly promising were followed by some clinical trials that were less conclusive. But finally it all came together and they were off and running. After almost twenty years of relentless effort, all the thrills and chills, all the ups and downs, the company finally went public and everyone in the company made at least a small fortune. David made a big one. One night he was over at the house and he seemed awfully down. He mentioned in an offhand manner that he had liver cancer, nothing to be done about it. He had a few months to live."

"Oh my God."

"But it wasn't dying young that depressed him. It was what he called the waste. He had spent the last twenty years of his life with a single-minded goal, the goal of going public and making all that money. Success. What had he been thinking? He made Tom Warson look well-adjusted. His two kids had grown up and he barely knew them. His wife had left him. He had put all his energy into that company. For what? For the Maserati he drove and the Lotus he kept in the garage? For the house on Lake Tahoe? What kind of legacy was that? And now it was too late to do anything about it."

"No one on his deathbed wishes he spent more time at the office," Ramon said, almost to himself. "Pretty bleak story. What can you say? There's nothing to say."

"We didn't think so, either. Then Kenny was talking to a friend of ours, Peter, a faculty member in the history department, a guy with heart disease who had been one of the first people to be treated with David's laser. We told him David was dying. Maybe he could write David a note and let him know what his treatment had meant to him. Instead, Peter and his wife invited David over for dinner. David offered to take them all out to the finest restaurant in the city, instead. But Peter insisted that David come to his house."

"So how'd it go?"

"That's what we asked him when he came over to tell us about it the next night. He said it went OK, if you call crying for three straight hours OK."

"What happened?"

"David showed up with a fancy bottle of wine, expecting a quiet evening at home with Peter and Claudia. Instead he walked into a dinner party with forty or fifty people.

Colleagues of Peter's from the history department. Friends from his church. A son who flew in from Los Angeles. A daughter from Boston. Nieces and nephews. Graduate students. People milled around, eating and talking. And then they sat David in a chair in the living room. One by one, people stood up and spoke through their tears about what it meant to have Peter—their friend and their teacher and their father and their husband—alive and healthy. And if that weren't enough, at the end of the night, after everyone had had their say and it was time for David to go home, every man woman and child in the room came over to David, gave him a hug that would last a lifetime and said two of the most magical words in the English language: Thank you."

"Beautiful."

"When David told Kenny and me what had happened, he looked at us in disbelief, shaking his head over and over. He just never imagined what he'd truly accomplished."

"But surely he knew. How could he not know?"

"How about you, Ramon? Do you ever think about how much pleasure you give people who love to watch you play tennis?"

"Not really. I know I have a few fans."

"More than a few. But how often do you think about the pleasure and delight that people get from watching you play? I asked David how many patients his company had treated over the last year. He choked up. He could barely get the answer out. Over four thousand, he finally whispered. I knew what he was thinking. He was imagining four thousand living rooms crowded with friends and family, glad to have someone they cherish, alive a little or a lot longer. The profits drove David Kornfeld to create that human delight and joy and gratitude. Not his good intentions. Not his introspection, sitting around thinking what he might be able to do to make the world a better place. I'm glad he didn't spend his time fly-fishing. So are the friends and families of four thousand people every year."

"Are all economists pro-business?"

"What do you mean?"

"You're always talking about how great high profits are. Are all economists pro-business?"

For the second time that day, Ramon saw Ruth struggle to keep her emotions in check. Very little frustrated her more than people misunderstanding how she felt about business and profits. But rather than respond right away, she took a deep breath and calmed down.

"I'm not pro-business. I'm not even pro-profits. There is nothing inherently good about high profits."

"But you just said—"

"It's a profit *and loss* system. I want bad businesses— businesses that are run poorly or dishonestly—I want bad businesses to lose money and let others use the freed-up capital and resources more wisely. Most entrepreneurs like David Kornfeld fail and that's fine. Let them. I don't want a company's profits to be artificially high, directing too much capital into that business. That's why almost all academic economists, myself included, oppose corporate welfare. The government should stop helping sugar farmers and corn growers and steel makers at the expense of taxpayers and usually consumers. Let corporations fend for themselves in competition with each other. It is the carrot of profit and the stick of loss that create wealth. And that carrot and stick only have meaning because of the prices that let people measure the value of something. Without the incentives of prices and profit and loss, you have no way of knowing what's truly valuable. Isn't it funny?"

"What?" Ramon said.

"Oscar Wilde said that a cynic is someone who understands the price of everything and the value of nothing. Clever people like to say the same thing about economists, as if we were soulless calculators in green eyeshades, obsessed with prices and money. We're mercenaries, it is said, weighing costs and benefits down to the last penny. But economics is not about prices and money. Economics is about how to get the most out of life. That's why I tell my students not to take the job that pays the most money. You should take the job that is most rewarding, where the rewards are monetary and nonmonetary. And to get the most out of life, you have to pay attention to costs and benefits. When you decided to come to Stanford, you ruled out the University of Miami. When you chose tennis, you gave up baseball. Doing homework with Amy is time you can't spend doing something else together. Everything has a price. Living life without taking account of the costs of what you do—the financial costs and the human costs, the costs you can measure and the costs you can only guess at—leaving those costs out of the picture is a sure way to live a meaningless life. When David Kornfeld chose to work on a laser, he lost the chance to work on some other invention. Thousands of people are glad he made that choice. And part of the reason he made that choice was because of a guess he made about the price that laser would fetch. Prices give us knowledge, knowledge that is impossible—impossible!—to have without those prices. In Amy's class, we talk about how the coordination of knowledge emerges from people's simple desire to buy and sell. Prices emerge and that lets—"

"I know. Prices let people around the world specialize. One company makes the cedar. Another makes the aluminum. No one knows how to make a pencil."

"Wow. How do you—"

"I usually get a synopsis within twenty-four hours. Actually, usually within twenty-four minutes. But don't tell Amy I told you."

"No problem. So, as people respond to prices and make their choices as buyers and sellers, knowledge flows around the world without anyone being in charge. But—"

"What do you mean, knowledge flows around the world?"

"The knowledge of how to produce a pencil is spread out around the world in people's heads. It isn't centralized in one place like a pencil factory or a government agency. And when something changes in the world that changes how many pencils people want to buy or how much graphite is available, buyers and sellers use a different kind of knowledge to cope with change. And that knowledge doesn't have to be centralized in one place, either. Pencils and tennis racquets and all the products that use graphite are out there waiting for us to enjoy them even though the smartest, most skilled person knows only a fraction of the knowledge that it takes to make them and a fraction of the knowledge about how to keep them in steady supply. It's an incredible thing we never notice."

"It's pretty amazing."

"The funniest thing is that economists don't know the price of everything. No one does. The whole system we call a market economy works as well as it does precisely because of how little we have to know. That leaves us free to focus on the few things we know and do well. Hayek called the system of prices that steer knowledge and resources, a 'marvel.' Have you heard of Hayek?"

"Yes, Amy again."

"But there's something equally amazing we haven't talked about yet in class. The prices don't just coordinate the knowledge dispersed among the buyers and sellers around the world. They create knowledge and expand it over time just like all those innovations in the egg business. Those innovations across the economy are the source of economic growth and prosperity—the source of that five- or ten- or fifteenfold increase in the standard of living of the average American. Who decides what is to be learned and discovered and improved? There's no technology czar. No committee of experts decides which innovations are more important than others. That might make you think that knowledge—the know-how and technology and engineering that create all the things we enjoy around us—just grows randomly as people figure out new stuff about the world. It's like this radio show I once heard. Callers had to answer twenty questions. If you could answer all twenty, you won two weeks in Hawaii. So I hear this caller who gets through and she's a genius. She gets the first question, then the second one, there's no stopping her. She nails the first sixteen questions like a machine gun mowing down cardboard cutouts."

"Easy questions?"

"The opposite. Impossible stuff. Obscure stuff. Capitals of countries you haven't heard of. Best Supporting Actress in 1948. Larry Bird's scoring average in his rookie year. She's blowing me away. But then the seventeenth question is just too tough. Name the first ten digits of Pi. She gets the first two and then she's making it up as she goes along. She's done.

So close. And I'm thinking, with the questions this hard, they'll never find anyone who can answer twenty straight. Then they take the next caller. And they ask him the same questions. And guess what? He knows Larry Bird's scoring average. He knows the capital of Burkina Faso. The first caller? She wasn't a genius after all. She'd been listening to all the other callers stumble on that first question until someone got it right and then they moved onto the next one until someone got that one right and then the next one. Any one caller wasn't so smart, but by relying on the knowledge of others and by paying attention, the later ones had knowledge they didn't have to uncover on their own. They leveraged the work of those who came before."

"Great story."

"It's half the story of the human quest for knowledge. The modern division of labor lets a person know very little and still look like a genius. That's why a person in the twenty-first century can be no brainier than a person a hundred years ago, yet a person today commands more knowledge, the accumulated knowledge of the previous hundred years. Just like the radio show makes the later callers look smarter than the ones who come before. And that's part of the reason a person today can make so much more money than a person yesterday. Ironically, the worker of today is more valuable than the worker of yesterday even though the worker of yesterday was more knowledgeable."

"Standing on the shoulders of giants. So why does the radio contest only capture half the story?"

"It captures the fact that we learn from those who came before us. But it misses how the questions get determined in the talk show of life. The talk show of life isn't about obscure trivia—there are prizes for figuring out stuff that changes people's lives. There's no host for the talk show of life asking the questions and setting the prizes. But you can still have questions and prizes without a host."

"So who hands out the prizes in the talk show of life?" Ramon found the idea both astounding and amusing.

"They hand themselves out."

"They hand themselves out," Ramon repeated. "How do they manage that?"

Ramon laughed and for a minute he was struck by how bizarre it was to be sitting and talking with the provost about prizes handing themselves out.

"Do you have time to get a cup of coffee?"

"I have time. Do you?"

"Sure." This lying thing was getting easier and easier, Ruth thought.

10

No Host No Problem

If only you could freeze time the moment before the Great Heart stopped beating and look around the nation and watch everyone in the last possible instant at the moment of before. Before everything would change, a man is leading a goat to milk it. He stops in mid-motion to pet its head. Before everything would change, a woman shakes a mop outside a window. A child is running in the street for no reason at all, just for the joy of running. At that instant, no one is aware that it is the last nanosecond of the Great One's life and that in another nanosecond, everything will change. Let time flow forward again and the man is stroking the goat's ears, the woman brings the mop back inside, the child stops to examine a beetle on the sidewalk. Nothing has really changed. Life goes on. But that is only a function of space and information. Life does not go on. Not for the Great Leader and not for the lives of his people. What will be changed by the silencing of his heart?

Ruth and Ramon walked over to an outdoor coffee place next to the library, not far from Ruth's office in the Economics department. On the way, Ruth asked Ramon about how his tennis practice was going and how he thought he might do this summer at Wimbledon. Their conversation and gestures and movement added to the feeling of vibrancy that made Stanford feel so alive, people walking, students on bikes seemingly swarming everywhere, whizzing miraculously at high speed without crashing into each other, weaving in and out of the people on foot like Ruth and Ramon, and in the middle of it all, groups of parents and students wandering here and there, getting a campus tour from a student volunteer. When they reached the café, Ruth paid for their coffees, and they sat down at a table across from each other.

"So tell me how the prizes hand themselves out," Ramon said.

"There are basically two ways to win the prizes—"

"The prizes that hand themselves out."

"Yes. Be patient. It really happens. If you can find a way to make something more effectively at a lower cost, your profits can go up. The higher profits are the prize. The eggs are an example of that. All that technology built into the hen house means higher profits for the innovator, at least for a while. Or you can come up with a new way of doing something that even though it's higher-priced, consumers still want to buy it. So you can actually win a prize by producing a product that's more expensive than the competition."

"For instance."

"An iPhone replaces an iPod which replaced a boom box. Eye surgery replaces contact lenses which replaced glasses. Antibiotics replace leeches. The bigger the improvement over what we already have, the higher the price you can charge relative to the existing products and the greater the profits. The bigger the prize. The more people that like what you've done also increases the prize. The prices and resulting profits are the way that creative people can get at what consumers would like them to work on without consumers having to convey that knowledge directly. Right now there are a whole bunch of unclaimed prizes out there. You come up with a battery for electronic devices that lasts a lot longer and you win a prize. You cure cancer, you get a big prize. You come up with wrinkle-free socks and you might win no prize at all. And not only is there no one to hand out the prizes, no one designed the system of profits and prices that lets consumers tell producers and innovators what they want."

"So where did that system come from if no one designed it?"

"It emerged. It sprung up. And because it works, it stays in place as long as we leave it alone. It is self-generating and self-sustaining."

"But if no one is in charge of the system, if there's no host, no Minister of Innovation, a lot of mistakes get made."

"Sure. People try and make shoes out of Corfam. They—"

"What's Corfam?"

"It's a synthetic leather. The inventors thought they'd invented sliced bread. They had solved two of the biggest problems of leather shoes—Corfam was waterproof and it never scuffed. You never had to shine Corfam shoes. Corfam was 'better' than leather. But consumers didn't like Corfam. They didn't like the way it looked. It looked like leather, but you could tell it wasn't really from a cow. Too shiny. Too perfect. And because it was so waterproof, Corfam shoes made your feet sweat."

"So Corfam turned out to be a waste."

"Yes. But that mistake was corrected. Corfam simply disappeared from the consumer market, although I understand it's still popular in the military. The clever people who had invented it, shrugged and tried to come up with something better."

"But that's a small mistake. What about the big mistakes that get made because no one's in charge? Look at all the resources that get wasted because businesses only care about profits."

"For example?"

"Look at cars. Why don't cars get better mileage?"

"How much should they get?"

"Carmakers could easily figure out a way for cars to get one hundred miles per gallon."

"Would two hundred miles per gallon be better?"

"Sure."

"Are you sure?"

"It's always better to use less gasoline than more."

"If that were true, then we should ban cars. That guarantees we'll use less gasoline. Life is about trade-offs. If we require carmakers to make cars that get better mileage, then we'll get lighter cars that are more dangerous to ride in. If we require the carmakers to keep the weight the same, we take away the incentive for carmakers to find ways to make lighter cars that use less aluminum or steel. What we really want is for carmakers to make more fuel-efficient cars only when it's worth it."

"But it's always worth it, isn't it?"

"No. A car might get 100 miles per gallon but if it costs $200,000 to produce it, it isn't worth it. No one would buy it because the cost of the technology would outweigh the savings in gasoline. Spending billions to develop a car that gets one hundred miles to the gallon is a mistake if gasoline costs a nickel a gallon or if there's a way to make cars run using sunlight instead of gasoline. Then all the effort and time to make a better mileage car would turn out to be wasted."

"OK, but in today's world, carmakers only want cars that get better mileage as long as people are willing to pay for it."

"Exactly."

"But the price of gasoline is too low. When people look at the savings from better mileage, it isn't worth it."

"Exactly."

"But that's the problem with economics. It makes everything a dollar and cents issue. Some things are more important."

"I couldn't agree more. But what do you have in mind?"

"Running out of oil. Using up the world's resources."

"But that's exactly what the dollars and cents are good for. If and when oil gets scarcer, the price will go up and encourage people to use less of it. If you ignore the price of oil and devote engineers and metal and other precious things to save gasoline, you'll save gasoline and waste other resources. You'll save gasoline by using up other stuff that's more valuable. Which is more important, oil or aluminum?"

Ramon thought for a moment.

"I'm not sure. They're both important. They're both finite."

"So which should we spend more resources on? Making cars that get better mileage or thinner soda cans?"

"Better mileage."

"What if the thinner cans saved millions of tons of aluminum but the better mileage only saved a few gallons of gasoline?"

"OK. I answered too quickly. I should have said it depends."

"And what does it depend on?"

"It depends on whether you save more aluminum or more oil."

"But how do you compare aluminum to oil? How much is one worth relative to the other? How would you decide? Weight?"

"No, but come on. It would be better to save a million barrels of oil than one ton of aluminum. It would be better to save a million tons of aluminum than a barrel of oil."

"Are you sure?"

"Yes."

"What if it took a million of the world's best engineers working for ten years to save a million barrels of oil, but you could save one ton of aluminum with an hour of an average engineer?"

"OK. So let's hold the number of engineers and their quality constant. It would be better to save a million barrels of oil using a thousand engineers if using the same number of engineers would save one ton of aluminum."

"Are you sure?"

"Why does that seem like a trick question?"

"Because it is one. Even if you had a choice between saving a million barrels of oil and a ton of aluminum using the same engineers, you still might want to save one ton of aluminum rather than a million barrels of oil."

"I'll bite," Ramon said smiling. "How could that possibly be?"

"Because we might be better off using those engineers to develop a solar-powered car, instead. Then saving the oil might be worthless. Or if we found a way to save a million tons of aluminum, it might not be worth it because we could have invented plastic soda bottles, instead. How do you deal with all the new innovation that comes along and changes the calculus of what something new is worth? What if it takes better engineers to save aluminum than oil? What if someone discovers a new oil field that's huge and cheap to exploit? The hostless radio show of innovation takes those things into account automatically using prices and profits. When aluminum gets scarcer, its price goes up and makes saving aluminum more profitable. If the engineers you need to make thinner cans are more expensive, then they cost the bottling company more money, making saving aluminum less attractive. If someone finds a way to make a plastic bottle, the demand for aluminum goes down, lowering the price of aluminum and making saving aluminum less attractive just as it should be. No Minister of Technology could possibly anticipate all the changes going on in the economy. No Innovation Czar could possibly master all the knowledge it takes to make wise decisions, even with a million computers. Better to let a thousand flowers bloom and let the best choices emerge from trial and error."

"Trial and error makes it sound random."

"It's not. It's just not perfectly planned. Genetic mutation is random. Natural selection accepts the good changes and rejects the bad ones. Economic evolution isn't random. Changes in products aren't random. The knowledge and innovation come from entrepreneurs trying to anticipate what people want and what will survive in the marketplace. That makes it more focused than biological evolution. And you get progress, not just survival. But most new businesses fail. Some fail because they're poorly executed. Others fail because the founders and the investors misread consumers or because the competition did something no one anticipated. How could any human mind or team of human minds organize the entire system? How could any human mind or team of human minds decide what was an improvement? Better to let prices and profits steer resources to where their value is the highest."

"But you admit that letting prices and profits steer resources doesn't always lead to the best outcomes."

"That's right. And not just the occasional mistake like Corfam that quickly disappears. Prices don't always include all the information you'd want them to include when they encourage or discourage some activity by going down or up. Driving pollutes the air that all of us breathe. The driver pays for the gas and the wear and tear on the car but ignores the toxins coming out of the tail pipe. The price of driving that emerges leads to too much pollution."

"That's called a market failure, right? I learned about that in my economics class."

"That's right. The people who call it a 'market failure' mean that in this situation, each person pursuing his or her own self-interest leads to outcomes we don't like."

"And government can improve things."

"It can. But the interesting question is not whether it can, but whether it will."

"Explain."

"Markets aren't perfect—the incentives that are provided by prices and profits aren't perfect. Giving people freedom to buy and sell doesn't always lead to perfect outcomes. Sometimes the competition that keeps prices low is slow in coming because of some barrier to entry. But why does it follow that government will make things better? The incentives that politicians face aren't perfect either. I assume some, maybe most, politicians want to make the world a better place. But I know it's not all they care about. Politicians also care about getting re-elected and about power. So they often respond to special interests rather than doing the right thing, especially when the right thing isn't well-defined or easy to observe. Corfam and the Edsel disappear quickly. The post office and ethanol subsidies and agricultural price supports and mediocre public schools live forever."

"But you admit that leaving people to their own devices can sometimes lead to disasters like pollution. And that sometimes government is necessary to improve the choices we make individually. Markets aren't perfect."

"They're not. And I'm not an anarchist. Government is good for lots of things. It's good for enforcing property rights and contracts. It can be good for cleaning up the air. Just don't romanticize politicians. They're human beings like the rest of us."

"But, Ruth, you romanticize the market!"

"Probably. But it deserves some romance."

"How do you figure?"

"It's hard to imagine the invisible hand. After all, it's invisible. Leaving things alone, leaving people to their own desires and dreams would seem like the last way to make the world a better place. So most people have a natural disposition for using the government to make things better. It would seem that managing something is always better than leaving something unmanaged. But it's not true. I think the world would be a better place if more people understood the virtues of unmanaged, uncoordinated, unorganized, undesigned action."

"I don't know, Ruth. It still seems like a mistake for society to make important decisions using only profits as the benchmark."

"Profits would be a terrible way to decide where to take a vacation or who to marry or how to spend your life. If you only use profits or money as the guideposts for your life, your soul will shrivel and die. What kind of moron marries the richest girl who'll take him? But an economy without profits or losses as guideposts will create a lot of suffering.

Even if David Kornfeld had been a saint, he wouldn't have spent the time he did on that laser without the profit motive. The work's too hard and the personal sacrifice is too great. You want another coffee?"

Ramon had jumped up from his seat. He shook his head, walking back and forth for a moment before sitting down again.

"I still think you romanticize profits a little too much," he said, ignoring her question. "It's easy to make the case for more lasers to fight heart disease. Or to talk in the abstract about knowledge or people figuring stuff out. That's all very nice. But you're ignoring how the profit motive destroys people's lives. Putting profits before people leads to downsizing and offshoring and outsourcing and all the things companies do in search of the almighty bottom line. Even the egg world you told me about where two people can take care of all those chickens means there are fewer jobs. That must be happening all over the economy."

"Oh, absolutely," Ruth said, delighting in his passion. "We make more cars and more steel and more eggs and more clothes using vastly fewer people than we did fifty or a hundred years ago. The essential economic story of the twentieth century is about workers becoming more productive. And one way you do that is by taking people out of the production process and substituting machines."

"So the whole process of wealth is driven by ruthlessness. You lower your costs by finding ways to get machines to do the work that people used to do. You survive in business by firing people. How can that possibly make the world a better place for anyone other than the businesses who make higher profits? You claim that prosperity is widespread. How can it be when workers are constantly losing their jobs to machines?"

"You're assuming the labor market is like musical chairs."

"Musical chairs? The kid's game?"

"Yes. Ten kids, say, are sitting in chairs arranged in a circle at a birthday party. You play some music. The kids get up and walk in the circle outside the chairs. While they're walking, you take away one of the chairs. When the music stops, you have to find a chair. But there aren't enough chairs to go around. That means more and more people shunted to the sidelines. My story about eggs makes the job market sound like musical chairs, doesn't it? The egg companies and the bottling plants and the car factories and the agribusiness corporations keep finding ways to reduce the number of workers you need to produce the goods. One less chair to sit in. Then another. Soon there just aren't enough chairs to go around. Next thing you know, there's an army of unemployed. Is that what you're saying?"

"And the losers have to sit on the outside of the circle where the lucky few catch a few crumbs from the privileged who get to eat the cake. Tell me what I'm missing."

"When a factory uses cleverly designed machines that reduce the number of workers needed to work in a factory, that means more stuff is made using fewer workers. That's an increase in productivity. But that in turn frees up resources to make things we didn't have before. So it's not just a question of products getting cheaper. It's the enormous explosion of new products and new services and the new job opportunities they create. The jobs in the computer industry that didn't exist *thirty* years ago, the jobs in entertainment, the jobs in health care. All the job categories that didn't exist *thirty* years

ago, let alone *a hundred* years ago. If you kept productivity unchanged, we simply wouldn't have enough people to
imagine, design, and produce all the new stuff."

"That's a nice story. But only people with jobs can afford
all that new stuff. How do you know the new jobs will equal
the ones that are lost? How do those old workers find the
skills to fill the jobs in those new opportunities?"

"Some don't. Some suffer. Some end up taking jobs that
pay less than the one they had before. But a lot of them end
up better off, with more choices than they had before. And
the next generation—the children of those workers who had
to cope with change—the next generation shapes the world
according to its dreams and its skills. The churn of employ-
ment creates opportunity. And the new opportunities greatly
outnumber the lost ones."

"Can you prove it?"

"I can. In 1900, America had about 30 million jobs. A
century later, we had over 130 million. Almost every year
there are more jobs in America than in the year before. A
hundred million new jobs in a hundred years! That process
involved an enormous amount of job destruction. A factory
lays off workers. Or doesn't replace the workers that retire
or quit. A factory shuts down and whatever it did moves to
Mexico or India. All those jobs lost. All those headlines in all
the local papers telling the story of those lost jobs. Fewer and
fewer chairs to sit in."

"Exactly. So where's the silver lining?"

"The labor market doesn't work like musical chairs. The
total number of jobs is mainly determined by the number
of people who want to work. And for most of the twentieth
century, more Americans wanted to work than had wanted

to before. So more jobs get created than destroyed in all but a few years of depression or recession. Look at what happened in the last half of the twentieth century when more women wanted to start working. Did they take chairs that used to belong to others? No. They brought their own chairs with them. Immigration surged in the last two decades of the twentieth century. Did unemployment soar? Were there fewer jobs for the people already here? No and no. It's the paradox of productivity. It's better to have two farmers looking after 800,000 chickens instead of a thousand farmers with smaller flocks. That frees up 998 farmers to go do something else to make the world a better place. As we destroy jobs, we get wealthier. The 998 farmers don't die and they don't starve. They find new jobs in new companies or in companies that are able to expand because eggs cost less."

"How do cheaper eggs create more jobs?"

"When people pay less for eggs, they have more money left over to spend on other things. That unspent money is a prize that hands itself out. That's why entrepreneurs, creative people, are always trying to come up with new things to claim those prizes. Without the cost-savings from eggs and millions of other products that have gotten cheaper, getting something new means giving up something old. When we make things more cheaply through either productivity or trade, that means we can have our cake and eat it too. We can have more eggs and more iPods and more artificial hips and everything else that makes life good."

"But who's the 'we'?" Ramon was getting angry. "Sure the rich get wealthier. But what kind of country is it, what kind of a brutal system punishes its poor that way—by putting them out of work to make the factory owners and the stockholders richer? It's despicable. The whole idea is morally bankrupt—throw people out of work so that stockholders and executives can make more money. OK, so maybe workers bring their own chairs. But the chairs have lower wages attached to them. Just to take one example—that laser to fight heart disease. Who can afford it? People with health insurance. But corporations like Big Box make sure that their employees can't afford health insurance. And why? Profits. Those profits you think so highly of. They force wages and benefits down. That's the price of those low prices you also like. The only way you get low prices is low wages. Your obsession with low prices has a hidden cost of low wages. That's why Big Box is so dangerous. That's where a lot of those out-of-work workers end up finding work."

"I thought you were upset with Big Box because of high prices."

"That night, the night of the earthquake, yes. But the rest of the time, their prices are too low. They're always pushing prices down."

"Sounds good."

"But they do that by pushing wages down."

"It's the other way around."

"What do you mean?"

"Retailers like Big Box or Wal-Mart have low prices because they've found a way for workers with relatively low skills and low wages to be productive. Competition forces them to pass the savings on to consumers. Their workers make less than the average worker in the economy because they don't have enough skills. If those chains didn't exist, do you think those workers would somehow magically have better jobs somewhere, working for nicer, less greedy employers?

Do you think that the workers in America who earn less than the median are the ones with bad luck who just happened to find themselves employed by the profit-hungry companies, while the other half are fortunate enough to work for the nice companies? If anything, Wal-Mart and the retailers who have been able to keep up with them—Target and Big Box and Costco—have increased the wages of low-skilled workers by increasing the demand for their services. Sam Walton created a business model that made low-skilled workers more productive. That increases their wages."

"Ruth, how can you tell me that the existence of Wal-Mart or Big Box is good for their workers? Don't you think that big retailers drive down wages in a quest for higher profits?"

"They'd like to. Just like every employee in every business, no matter how generous or loving or cruel or rapacious, would prefer to make more. They'd like to. But they can't. How could they?"

"Are you going to tell me they don't drive down prices?"

"That they do. And those lower prices have helped millions of customers, many of them poor. A company can lower prices below the competition or raise its wages above the competition. But it can't freely raise prices. Or lower wages. It will lose customers and workers. It's like me trying to charge a premium if I were selling my house just because I wanted to make more money for my retirement."

"Amy told me about that. But you're just one home-owner. Wal-Mart is huge."

"Not really. They only employ a little over a million or so employees."

"Only a million." Ramon looked incredulous. "You're saying that's a small number?"

"As big a number as that seems, it's only about 1 percent of the work force in America. If there were 'only' a hundred houses for sale in Palo Alto, do you think that would let me charge a premium for my house because there were only ninety-nine alternatives competing with mine? If Wal-Mart pays less than its competitors, who would work there? When Wal-Mart opens a new store, people line up for the opportunity. Why? Why would people line up to be oppressed? A lot of the people who work there think it's a good job. For them it is."

"You're the only person I know who thinks Wal-Mart is good for America."

"No, I think the process that produces Wal-Mart is good for America."

"Same thing, isn't it?"

"Not at all. If Wal-Mart can't meet its competition's quality and prices, I want it to go out of business. Which it probably will some day, just like many of its competitors before it."

Ramon stopped to think about how that might possibly be true. Ruth stopped to watch a hummingbird hover for an instant over the hedge across the way before it zipped off in search of sweetness somewhere else.

"OK," Ramon said, "suppose I accept your point. There are still a lot of people working for Wal-Mart who don't make a lot of money. What would you do to help them?"

"I know what I wouldn't do. I wouldn't shut down Wal-Mart or keep them from expanding or force them to pay higher wages or health benefits. Those ideas, even when they're well-intentioned, will end up hurting the people you're trying to help by making it more costly to hire workers. And they're not always well-intentioned. Most of the impetus for those moves comes from competitors who want to handicap a successful rival. That's a bad option to offer a company— instead of finding a better way of pleasing your customers, spend your time in Washington or your state capitol trying to convince politicians to give you an artificial advantage. Besides, the whole thing is really backwards. Instead of forcing or lobbying Wal-Mart to pay more, we ought to look for ways to make low-skilled workers more skilled. That's a better way to help people who struggle to make ends meet."

"And in the meanwhile?"

"In the meanwhile, things are better than you think. Even the poor are sharing in the prosperity. Do you have a minute to come by my office? We can look at the data. I think it'll surprise you."

Ruth knew this was a gamble, but she took a chance that Ramon was still interested. To her delight, he said yes. They walked to her office—not the provost's office where she knew the puzzled and maybe angry phone messages would be piling up about her missed meetings, but her office over at the Economics department. The two of them sat in front of the computer and Ruth showed Ramon the studies on inequality and mobility and whether people were getting better off or worse off. She showed him how people on either side of the political spectrum could distort the debate by choosing either family income or household income or wages or compensation or by choosing the right starting date for the analysis or by ignoring inflation or mis-measuring it. When it was over, Ramon had received a pretty good introduction on how statistics get used and abused. Finally, after a good hour of questions and answers, Ramon rose to leave.

"Can I ask you one more question?" he asked.

"Ask two more."

The phone rang. Ruth gave it a quick look and turned back to Ramon, letting him know she wasn't going to answer it.

"If I understand what you've told me today, the United States has achieved the standard of living it has today because profits and prices give entrepreneurs and creative people an incentive to discover new stuff that people value. Is that a fair summary?"

"Couldn't have said it better myself."

"So if technology and knowledge are the keys to prosperity, why aren't all nations equally rich? Cuba and Ghana and Syria and Peru can buy those same computerized chicken coops you told me about. Technology is available everywhere. But some nations are poor and some are rich. If competition pushes prices down to benefit consumers, why aren't Mexican consumers rich? Why does my mom have a higher standard of living in the United States than she did in Cuba?"

The kindling had caught. He wasn't angry any more. He was curious. He wanted to understand. Ruth wanted to take his face in her hands and kiss him. But she restrained herself and merely gave him a smile.

"If I knew the answer to those questions," she said, "I'd have a Nobel Prize. But I can tell you the beginning of an answer. The wealthy nations have more capital. More physical capital, machines and factories and computers. The people in those wealthy countries have more human capital, more knowledge and the skills to work with the physical capital. The wealthy countries have policies that encourage risk-taking and the accumulation of both kinds of capital. Economics and political power are dispersed in the wealthy countries.

The poor countries are more likely to be run by thugs who take what they can. Think Cuba or Syria. That discourages the accumulation of physical or human capital. That discourages foreign investment that might make the workers more productive. The presence of thugs discourages risk-taking. The poorer countries are more likely to have concentrated economic interests that fight any changes that might bring competition. Think of the retail sector in Japan or the whole economy in places like Argentina. Do you know Argentina in 1920 was one of the richest countries in the world? What went wrong? People like to worry that the rich make all the rules in America, but those are people who have never studied a country like Argentina. If I had to guess, I'd guess that the richest families in Argentina in 1920 are still doing well today and that they're as well off as the richest Americans. The difference is that there aren't very many of them. They fought all the changes that might have spread the wealth through competition. The rich countries have more open borders to products and services and people. The poor countries are more likely to restrict trade. Self-sufficiency is the road to poverty. It is better to leverage the skills of others and buy what you cannot make effectively on your own. The rich countries have the rule of law, where a person can buy something or enter a deal and know that the fruits of that deal won't be arbitrarily stripped away. And on top of all of that, the rich countries have a culture of trust where everything doesn't have to be put into a contract. But if I had to sum it up in a single thought, the rich countries have more freedom. More freedom to innovate, freedom to compete, freedom to take risks, freedom to fail. Freedom to compete, freedom to trade, freedom to—"

The phone rang again and this time, Ruth looked at her watch. It was almost two o'clock. They had talked through lunch. She had missed even more meetings than she had expected. And there was a limit to how long even the most curious student could keep talking and thinking economics. Maybe it was best to give Ramon a break. She picked up the phone.

"Ruth Lieber."

There was a flood of words from the other end, Ruth's assistant in the provost's office. Was she all right? Where had she been? Was her cell phone broken? The governor was expecting to see her at two o'clock and what was she going to tell him if Ruth weren't there and on and on.

The governor. Class of '80. Fine fellow. Not as entertaining as his predecessor, but she was always happy to see him. Of course she'd be there—she could get to her other office in maybe three minutes if she hustled. She hung up and took a deep breath and looked again at her watch. Four minutes to two.

"Ramon. Something's come up. I need to go. But here are a few books you can have." She quickly moved among the shelves and pulled down three books.

"I shouldn't—" he began.

"Take them. They're yours. I'll be boxing them up anyway, trying to find a home for them soon enough." She waved her hand, taking in the whole room.

"I can't," he began again but she shoved them at him.

"Stay as long as you want," she said, heading out the door. "Just close the door when you're done. Sorry I have to run," she called back to him, already halfway down the hall. As soon as she turned the corner, she started running for the stairs. No need to make the governor wait. She tried to think of what she could tell the president of the university if he discovered she'd spent half the day ignoring her responsibilities. A senior moment? A series of senior moments? She decided she'd just tell the truth—she'd been working with a student. For four hours? Well, he wasn't an ordinary student. That explanation would have to do. He'd never believe her if she told them what she really had in mind.

11

The Weaver of Dreams

The chest no longer rises and falls, the monitors flatline and for an instant, only the doctors know what has happened. They hesitate in the sudden silence and everything truly does stop around the bedside for that instant. Then the doctors whirr back into life like a car engine responding to the ignition key on a cold morning. Once the moment of silence and suspension has passed, the news begins to swell outward, pounding on the shore of the nation like a great storm.

As news of the death of the Great Leader spreads, minds and tongues are in motion, trying to figure out what has changed and what is the same. The man who collects and sells parts for the 1960s cars tries to imagine what he could possibly do instead. The woman peeling potatoes for the restaurant she runs in her living room imagines opening a real restaurant. The boy with the magic hands, the boy who has tamed a thousand basketballs over a thousand afternoons, dreams of going to college in America. The manager of the state-run hotel catering to the Europeans wonders if he'll still have a job in a year and if he does, whether the work will be harder or easier. The Minister of the Interior in charge of prisons has a sudden urge to do something quieter and less lucrative.

Life after college is like tennis, Ramon thought to himself, cringing at the very thought of having such a silly thought. You have to know when to go to the net and when to play the baseline. Life after college is like tennis. You have to keep your eye on the ball. Worse. Much worse. Maybe it's like a tennis tournament. Whether you have a high seed or a low seed, you always have a chance. That's a lie. Life is like the locker room before a tennis match. Even the greatest player puts his pants on one leg at a time. So it is in the great locker room of life—we should treat each other as equals. Equals in our underwear, stepping into our pants. Beautiful. Now he was really on a roll. Maybe life is nothing like tennis. In tennis, love is zero, but in life, love is everything. Would that work? No, it's horrible, he thought. It's worse than horrible.

It was Friday morning. Graduation day was Sunday and Ramon couldn't figure out how to end his graduation speech. He was happy enough with the rest. It would make trouble for Ruth Lieber, but he couldn't see any way around that. Why couldn't he stop thinking about this old woman he hardly knew who had talked to him a handful of times? There was no way he could give in to her. There was no way he could repudiate what he believed in just to please her. Still, his speech was a chance to redeem what had happened at the protest, a chance to purge the taint of dirty money from his university. Finally, he'd be in control without the shenanigans of Heavy Weather and his friends.

Forget the ending. He still had a couple of days. Maybe a bike ride would clear his head. Give the speech a rest and work on the hills, instead. He headed west on Page Mill Road, on his way to a park in the hills above Palo Alto. It was a brutal ride, but the view from the top was worth it. He attacked the road and ripped his way to the top of the ridge that separates the Bay from the sea. Soon enough, the relentless effort pushed his thoughts away from protests and prices and even Ruth Lieber. At the top, he found the park and headed for the bench at the vista he and Amy liked to admire, high above the Bay, the university below him, the Hoover Tower visible and then the water and the bridges and the hills on the other side across the water. He felt his cell phone vibrate and looked down to see his mother's caller ID. She must be calling to confirm her flight for tomorrow.

"Hey, Mama. What's happening," he said in Spanish.

All he could hear on the other end was static interrupted by his mother shouting something into the phone over and over again. Music in the background blurred everything together.

"I can barely hear you. Are you all right?"

"He's dead! He's dead!" she screamed.

"Who's dead?" Oh, God. Uncle Eduardo. He'd been sick. Ramon pulled off the road. "I'm sorry, Mom. I'm so sorry."

"Sorry? Why are you sorry? He's dead! Castro is dead!"

"Castro! I thought it was Uncle Eduardo."

"Uncle Eduardo? He's right here getting drunk and dancing."

They talked for a while, a surreal conversation, Ramon three thousand miles away, in this serene landscape seemingly untouched by the change that was rocking his mother's world and the world of all his relatives. When he finished talking with his mother, he sat for a while. Then he got back on his bike and headed for home.

Ramon's cell phone vibrated again. He looked down. Amy.

"Hey."

"Are you all right?"

"What's wrong?" She sounded upset, almost frantic. "Why wouldn't I be all right?"

"Where are you?"

"I'm on my bike. About thirty minutes from home. Where are you?"

"I'm standing outside your apartment. I came by to get a book I left there last night and I can't get near the front door. The street is swarming with people and campus police and TV crews, those vans with the big antennae. Fox is here. CNN. ESPN. All the networks. Every local station has a truck here. You sure everything's OK? Any idea why all these people are camped on your doorstep?"

"Can't imagine. Haven't won any tennis tournaments lately or spoken at any protests. It's just a typical, ordinary day. Except Castro died. My mother just called. She couldn't stop—"

"That's it."

"What?"

"The TV crews. The people on your front steps, in the street. They're waiting for you. They want a reaction."

"Why would they want to talk with me? I'm a Stanford student who plays tennis. Who cares what I think? My mother's a different matter. She could give them a good quote. But I have nothing to do with Castro. I left the island when I was five. All those people must be there for some other reason. Maybe that guy in the apartment upstairs went off the deep end and—"

"Ramon. Wake up. Don't you see? You're the most famous Cuban in the world. Or at least the most famous living one. It used to be that guy with the beard and a cigar. But he's gone now. You're it. After the president of the United States, you're the man they're all going to want to talk to."

There was a long silence on the other end of the line. At first, Amy thought maybe Ramon's phone had cut out in the hills. Then she heard him breathing as he stood on the pedals and punished the bike forward, taking in her argument and knowing she was right.

"Can we get together? Someplace quiet where I won't be easily recognized."

She thought for a moment.

"Baylands."

"Perfect. I'll be there in about forty-five minutes. Only the hawks know me there. Meet you at the nature center."

On a weekday morning, Amy and Ramon had the marsh to themselves. The swallows danced and darted, oblivious to the only two people walking through the marsh. Ramon and Amy leaned on the railing of the observation deck that sat in the middle of the marsh, looking out toward the hills across the Bay.

"So how do you feel?" Amy asked.

"Weird. I've never thought much about Castro. My mom hates him. Hated him," Ramon corrected himself before continuing. "My mom hated him but I always figured that my dad must have thought he was okay or he wouldn't have stayed."

"Did your mom tell you that?"

"No. She doesn't like to talk about it. Maybe it was something they fought over. I've always wondered whether it had something to do with me."

"Put yourself in your father's shoes. You're beloved by the people. Closely watched by the government. You have a young wife. Soon you have a young wife who's expecting a child. Would you want to move to a new country?"

"Only to find out if I could get around on a major league fastball."

"And that would matter a lot. But so would those other things. I'm not sure you can tell much from knowing that he stayed. How often do you think about your dad?"

"Not that often. Just every day."

Amy took his hand. They were quiet now, watching the birds.

"Do you ever wonder what your life might have been like if your mom had stayed in Cuba?"

"Sure. There are a lot of things I don't like about America. But there are so many things here I could never have experienced back in Cuba."

"Such as?"

"Tennis, for one. Tennis isn't a priority there. I probably would have been a baseball player. Or who knows. I might have gotten involved in track. Would I have enjoyed it? Probably. But I doubt I'd have liked it as much as tennis."

"Anything else?"

"Life is easier here. Sometimes I worry about whether it's too easy. But I know easy is often very good."

"Anything else?"

"Like what?" he said, smiling.

"Oh, I don't know. Anything at all. Better dental floss here in America. I'm sure you can think of something else here in America that you wouldn't have if you grew up in Cuba."

"Can't think of a thing," he said, turning toward her and kissing her, a long lingering kiss. "Well, other than the blondes," he added, finally. "Blondes named Amy. You just don't find that many blondes named Amy in Havana."

"So what do you think will happen in Cuba now?" Amy asked. "Do you think things will change? What do you want to see happen? Do you want to talk about it to the press or at graduation? That's what people are going to want to hear from you."

"Hard to know what will happen next. It feels like a turning point. Maybe. If things really do change, if somehow, some kind of freedom comes to Cuba, I wonder if my mom would think of moving back."

"And you?"

Ramon shrugged. The whole thing was too surreal.

"Hard to imagine. Meanwhile, I have a slightly more pressing dilemma. What should I do about that crowd waiting at my place?"

"I have no idea. But I think I know someone who can help."

Ruth Lieber was drinking coffee on her patio, trying to finish up the past Sunday's *New York Times Magazine* crossword puzzle, while she waited for a phone call she was expecting. Five letters, Mexican actress. She had no idea. Maybe she needed to get out more. Her mind wandered to her favorite tennis player and his upcoming graduation speech. The Stanford president had called earlier to remind her that Bob Bachman would be in town to watch his daughter graduate. Was Ruth planning on getting together with him while he was in town to close the deal on that new interdisciplinary center?

His daughter! Ruth had forgotten about Cordelia Bachman. What a mess. If Ramon Fernandez used his speech to stick a knife into Big Box with Bob Bachman sitting in the crowd, she could kiss that next Big Box donation goodbye. And any more down the road. What was she going to do about it? Well, it was only money. OK, it was a lot of money. But she couldn't think of any way out of this one.

Besides, she had come to think the world of Ramon Fernandez. He was better company than Bob Bachman. Plus he had the potential to be at least as influential an alum as a CEO like Bachman. At least that's what she told herself when trying to justify her inaction. Leaving him alone was really a no-brainer. Just forget about it, she told herself. Back to the Mexican actress, first letter an H. Nothing. She put the puzzle down and saw Ramon Fernandez coming through the side yard, Amy at his side.

"Sorry to intrude," Ramon said. "No one answered the phone or the front door."

"Are you guys OK?" Ruth figured something extraordinary must have happened to prompt an unannounced visit.

"Castro's dead," Amy said.

"I know. Saw it on the Internet."

"It's created a little bit of a problem for Ramon."

Amy explained the media crush at Ramon's apartment.

"It's complicated my life, too," Ruth said. "Though you can see it's a little quieter here."

"What's wrong?" Amy asked.

"Our main commencement speaker may not make it. She's a former secretary of state. The president wanted to see her about Cuba. Not the president of Stanford. *The* President. Something about a 'window of opportunity.' She went. I don't blame her. She can't promise she'll be back in time. I'm waiting for a phone call from her right now."

"What are you going to do?"

"I told the president—of Stanford that is—that we should just go with our student speaker and give him a little more time. He's got plenty of star power and everyone wants to hear what he has to say, anyway. Can you handle being the headliner? I figure you're used to it. And I figure your speech is already written. It is written, right?"

"Most of it. I've been struggling with how to end it. This solves my problem. I'll add something about Castro and Cuba. As long as I don't have to talk twice as long." Ruth shook her head. "My biggest problem right now is getting into my apartment," Ramon said.

"Why don't you schedule a press conference at the admin building for this afternoon, say two o'clock. That's what— three hours away? That will give you time to think of what you want to say and prepare a statement. The evening news people will be happy because they'll have the tape they need for tonight. I'll send someone from media relations over to your apartment to spread the word. That should dispel some of the crowd."

"I probably ought to change into something a little nicer than sweats if I'm going to hold a press conference. But I've got a change of clothes at the tennis center that'll do."

"Let's get you some help with your statement. Let me call Jeff Jacobson. He's the university's chief communications guy."

"You don't have to do that. He doesn't have to do that. It's my problem. I can handle it. At least I think I can."

"I'm sure you can. But look. Castro's death is going to lead the news tonight. There'll be interviews with someone from the State Department or the White House. Some man-on-the-street stuff with people in Little Havana. And there's going to be something from you. Your talking head is going to be seen on a lot of television sets. Underneath that talking head is going to be your name. Underneath your name, it's going to say Stanford University. That makes it part of Jeff's job. He's good. Very good. He can help you walk the finest of lines you might want to take. Trust me."

Ramon realized that he did.

"Come on," she encouraged. "I'll go in with you. I've got some graduation details to take care of with Jeff, anyway."

With Jacobson's help, Ramon crafted an opening statement for the press conference. Then Jacobson drilled Ramon on the type of questions he thought the press would ask. When they were done practicing, Ramon stopped by Ruth's office and thanked her for the help.

"My pleasure, Ramon. I'm going to miss talking with you. Watching you win tournaments on TV just won't cut it."

"Always the optimist. I appreciate your confidence. I'll miss you, too."

"Stay in touch. Drop me an e-mail when you have a chance to read any of those books I gave you." She looked down at her watch. "Well, you better go. You've got to be back here by 2."

She was right. He had to get going. But something about the mood he was in made him ask the question that had been bothering him.

"Professor Lieber, why have you been talking to me these past few weeks? Why have you made me one of your students?"

She smiled. She hadn't expected the question but she had thought he might be wondering. She took a deep breath.

"I wanted you to understand something of possibility and prosperity. We human beings are very different from other animals."

"Yes, we play tennis and they don't. We study economics and they don't. We . . ."

"I was actually thinking of something a little more interesting. We dream and they don't. We imagine. We look to the future in a way that lets us plan. We save. We invest. We forego pleasure today for something greater tomorrow and we understand why we're doing it. Jonas Salk dreams of curing polio or Fred Smith dreams of a way to get a package to someone overnight or Steve Jobs dreams of a way to carry 20,000 songs in your pocket or Tom Warson makes that golden widget that sustains the Internet or David Kornfeld takes a laser and finds a way to save lives with it. And it's not just the entrepreneurs doing the dreaming. We dream, too. Just to take one example, millions of Americans now try to lead healthier lives than they did in the past. They decide to exercise more and eat better. Think of the enormous range of things that have to happen and that do happen to let those plans and dreams come to reality. New kinds of food in the grocery store. New kinds of grocery stores. New kinds of running shoes and racquetball shoes and walking shoes. New kinds of clothes made of new materials that make sweating more pleasant. New kinds of exercise machines. Videos to go with them. New kinds of bikes. More tennis rackets. New kinds of tennis rackets. People to make all those things and work in all those places making and selling and explaining to people about the new choices that are available. An enormous army of workers and creators springs into action. The plans of all the people who want to eat better and exercise more got matched with the plans of all the entrepreneurs who strove to make money meeting those desires."

"That's a good thing, sure," Ramon interjected. He didn't see what she was getting at.

"But who made sure that those dreams and desires, those plans and actions didn't conflict with each other or with the thousands of other dreams and plans under way at the same time? All the resources—the workers and the raw materials—that had to be mobilized to make sure that life elsewhere in the economy wasn't hopelessly disrupted? Who settled those disputes over how much land would be devoted to organic food and how much to junk food? Because there's more and better junk food, too. What a world we live in. You can get organic milk and four kinds of mesquite flavored potato chips! The dreams of a healthier America didn't shut down the dreams of those who wanted to be couch potatoes playing video games. Some biochemists even figured out ways to reduce the cholesterol of the couch potatoes so they wouldn't pay too high a price for not exercising. Who made sure there were enough biochemists and enough engineers working on the lasers? Who made sure that Nike would find all the rubber and fabric and workers it needed to cushion the feet of all those runners while other shoemakers were looking for materials and workers because a TV show made higher heels all the rage? Who let David Kornfeld develop that laser while laser tag parlors were opening at the same time? How is there seemingly always plenty of the things we want? And all without fights and chaos and turmoil? What is the source of the unseen harmony around us?"

Ramon said nothing. Her passion silenced him. He waited for her to go on.

"Who is the weaver of dreams?" Ruth continued. "Who makes sure that all the dreams can coexist peacefully? Who weaves together all the plans to make sure that they work in parallel rather than producing conflict?"

"I don't know. I have a feeling from our earlier conversations that there isn't one."

"That's right. There isn't one. Each of us takes the unique strands of our hopes and dreams and adds them to everyone else's. Yet, somehow they all fit together and the tapestry of our lives just gets more interesting and varied and human. But how do our choices manage to fit together without a weaver of dreams? How is it that some of us can become vegetarians or exercise fanatics or couch potatoes or take up the guitar or become gardeners or engineers or teachers and all the products and tools we need are out there waiting for us without us having to let anyone know what we're going to choose? How is it that 100 million Chinese can leave the countryside and their kids start using pencils and bicycles but there's still graphite for that magic wand you wield on the tennis court? Who sends out the memo to put all the effort into motion to make sure all the dreams can coexist so peacefully?"

"No one does, Ruth. I've learned that from you. But I don't know how it manages to happen."

"The prices. Our choices fit together because the price of everything can adjust and steer resources and knowledge throughout the economy. In a course like Amy's, we learn about how the prices do their magic. You and I didn't have time for that. But we did have time for you to see a glimpse of the magic. We only see our own little corner of the tapestry. No one can see the whole thing. But the genius of the system is that our little corner is all we need to see. No one has to know the price of everything even though the price of everything is always adjusting in response to all the changes going on in our incredibly dynamic economy. The graphite owner can focus on the price of graphite and spend the rest of the time learning about how to find cheaper ways of getting graphite out of the ground. And because no one has to know the price of everything, our knowledge grows, our world gets better, and no one has to master all the dreams going all at once to make sure they somehow fit together. I wanted you to understand something of that, something of the poetry of the possible."

Once again, Ramon studied the face of the woman in front of him. Ramon saw nothing there suggesting guile, strategy, or manipulation. Was she trying to help him the way she had claimed before the protest—spare him embarrassment, by steering him from the wrong path in that speech she never mentioned? Why wouldn't she just come out and say it, straight out? Was she just afraid that if she said it explicitly it would merely strengthen his resolve to stick to his principles? Maybe there was something deeper going on, something he sensed but couldn't grasp. He couldn't help but wonder what dreams she was weaving.

"I wanted you to understand," Ruth went on, "that not everything glorious that we observe in the world around us is the result of someone's intention. There is wonder in the world that we humans create without any one of us fully understanding it. Appreciating that is part of being an educated person. Someday you'll be glad to know about it."

"Someday or Sunday?" he asked, trying to get to what was pushing her so hard.

"Sunday? What do you mean, Sunday?" She stopped, confused. Then she understood. She started laughing. "Did you think the time I've been spending with you has something to do with your speech on Sunday?" Ramon was totally bewildered. Either she was a total mystery to him or the greatest actress who never appeared on screen or stage.

"I don't care about Sunday," Ruth said, shaking her head and regaining her composure. "Except that you give a good speech. Say whatever you want. Speak from the heart. Otherwise, you'll fall flat, like most graduation speakers. Speak from the heart."

What a woman, he thought. In one sense, she was simply practicing what she preached. Leaving things alone. But Ramon knew that leaving things alone wasn't Ruth Lieber's only strategy in life. He knew from Amy how hard she prepared for her classes. She didn't expect her lectures to emerge without lots of planning. Even her stories of the economy having an unplanned orderliness about it had people within their own part of the economy planning and using the information available to them. So what was she doing? Instead of stopping him from giving his speech, it looked like she was giving him an even bigger stage. Did she agree with him in some sense and feel that taking money from Big Box was a mistake even while she disagreed with him about the wisdom of letting prices work in the aftermath of a catastrophe? He didn't know what to think. But he knew that her advice to speak from the heart was genuine. He'd do the best he could. He still needed an ending.

Ramon headed to the tennis center for his change of clothes. He opened his locker and saw a post-it note, taped to the top shelf. On the note was a big arrow pointing to the bottom of the locker. At the bottom of the locker was a package and a card. He opened the card. "Dear Ramon, Happy Graduation, With respect, Ruth Lieber."

Ramon smiled and opened the package. It was a book, but to his surprise, it was a collection of poems by Mary Oliver and not the economics treatise on emergent order he expected. On a bookmark, Ruth had written, "Don't miss this one." Ramon sat down on the bench in front of his locker and read the poem. Then he read it again. Maybe it was an economics book after all.

12

A WILD AND PRECIOUS LIFE

With the casket lowered into the ground and the rifles blazing in salute, it really did appear that the Great One was mortal after all. The speeches went for hours, all dutifully covered by the state television network. There was no dancing in the streets, though some rum was hoisted in private dwellings, late at night, with the shades drawn.

Had anything really changed? Would all the power and authority remain at the top? Or would others begin to have a say—that charismatic General, the editor of that newspaper some said was funded secretly by the United States, the Minister of Agriculture who seemed to be a decent fellow, who understood sugarcane but little of politics, the cousin of Castro who some said was in favor of reform? Who would matter now? The same people or could something really be different now that Castro was gone?

Could change come to Cuba? It was all the Cuban-American community in Miami talked about on the phone, in their houses over dinner, in bars, at restaurants. It was all the Cuban-American community in San Francisco and Washington, D.C. and New York talked about. And after people tired of talking about the chances for democracy or even just a little more freedom, a bigger question lurked in the background, the question of going home.

Ruth Lieber woke early on graduation day. She pulled up her e-mail and looked over the final version of the schedule for the day that her assistant had sent her late the night before. The day kicked off with breakfast with Bob Bachman and the dean of Arts and Sciences. She wasn't sure how to handle that. Warn Bachman of what was coming later? Let events take their course? Maybe Ramon's speech would turn out to be harmless. But if Ramon gave a rabble-rousing speech that vilified Big Box, then Bachman would be doubly furious. She decided to roll the dice and play it cool. If Ramon's speech turned out well, she was pretty sure that Bachman would come through with the big gift. If Ramon's speech was a disaster, no amount of prepping Bachman for the worst would salvage things. Besides, Bachman's daughter would be joining them. That would probably work to keep things calm.

Ramon also woke early. Ruth Lieber had handed him the solution for ending his speech. But the speech didn't work the way he wanted it to. Adding on a few words about Castro and Cuba seemed artificial. The segue from the first part, the part he had already written, seemed forced. What was that advice in freshman comp? Something about killing your darlings. He had to make it better.

Ruth's breakfast went swimmingly. Of course, Bachman hadn't seen the program yet. He didn't know that Ramon was speaking and Ruth hadn't told him. Much of the time at breakfast was taken up by conversation with his daughter, Cordelia, who was a very pleasant young woman, disproving both genetic and environmental theories of human behavior.

After breakfast, Ruth went over to the stadium to make sure things were under control. It was totally unnecessary—her staff was superb—but Ruth liked the atmosphere in the stadium on commencement day. She liked to watch the stadium fill up. She liked to look at the faces of the parents, radiating pride and delight that their children had made it through. And she liked to look at the faces of the students, still the children of those parents, but ready to fly into whatever life had to offer.

Then the ceremony began. The president of the university welcomed the parents, then introduced Ramon to the crowd. Ruth couldn't help noticing out of the corner of her eye that Bob Bachman was trying to get up out of his seat so that he could storm out, but his wife held onto his upper arm firmly and whispered something in his ear, probably something about their daughter. Ruth sat calmly and found herself thinking not about Big Box or price gouging but about teaching and the economics of investment.

Ruth's favorite metaphor for investment was the planting of a seed. A planted seed has value long before it becomes a tree. The potential benefits are enough to give it value. Teaching is the planting of seeds. Knowledge, or even better, wisdom, is an investment like a tree that goes on and on producing fruit. But unlike a fruit tree, you have no idea when the fruit will come or what kind it will be. Ruth had no idea whether anything of her teaching would affect the speech she was about to hear. There might have to be a lot more rain and sunshine for that to happen. She had no idea whether that speech would hurt her or help her with Bob Bachman, but either way, she felt in her bones that something she had taught Ramon would come to good sometime, somewhere. She held on to that thought as Ramon stepped to the microphone.

"As I was coming up on stage," Ramon began, "the president told me to break a leg. I told him to be careful what you wish for. The last speech I gave on campus I almost did break a leg."

The crowd laughed. Ruth relaxed a little. Even Bachman smiled.

"Today's ceremony is called commencement," Ramon continued. "I've always enjoyed the irony of that title. For most of us, today is the reminder of what is ending—our time here on this beautiful campus, a place where we arrived four years ago, so unsure of what lay ahead. Oh, some of us thought we knew what lay ahead, but life has a way of surprising you. You make your plans. You hold onto your dreams as best you can, but often, things beyond your control change everything."

Ramon paused and looked to his right, where Ruth Lieber was sitting on the stage behind him. Did he wink at her? It looked that way to Ruth.

"I once heard a lesson when I was fifteen that stuck with me, and I'd like to share it with you today. It was a hot September afternoon in Miami and I was at tennis practice. We were doing some conditioning drill and we were dying. The coach called us over and we knelt on the grass on one knee, panting, chests heaving, sweating. Coach gave us some kind of pep talk. I've forgotten most of it. It was probably something about when the going gets tough, the tough get going. But at the end he said something I'll never forget. At the end he said, 'You honor your parents by what you become.'

"What he meant was that rather than honoring your parents by what you say to them or how you treat them, although that's important, too, you honor your parents by the life you choose to lead. That's what they ultimately care about. That is their reward. So what will we become, as we begin this journey of life after college?"

Ramon stopped and let the question hang in the air.

"The other night I was watching a movie, *The Truman Show*. Jim Carrey plays Truman Burbank, an unwitting, unaware star of the longest running reality show. He thinks he lives a normal life, but everyone he encounters, from his best 'friend' to his wife to the man behind the counter at the corner newsstand, is actually an actor under the direction of the show's mastermind, Christof. Truman has been watched by billions on television since his birth. He has a Christof-induced fear of water that keeps him from leaving what he thinks is an island, but which is in fact a gigantic stage where his life runs its course.

"The movie takes place during a time when Truman starts to wonder if his life is really real. At one poignant moment, the woman he is talking to is wearing a button that says, 'How's it going to end?' To Truman it's just a weird button, but for us, the viewers, it's particularly poignant because we know it's a button that fans of the show wear and the 'it' is Truman's life.

"How's it going to end? What will we become? That question hovers in the air around us, around our lives. And finally, Truman, in an act of great courage, gets in a little boat and decides to escape from the island where he was born to discover what is beyond the sea." Ramon paused and looked to the section of the stadium where he knew his mother was sitting. "Such courage does not only take place in the movies, in Hollywood.

"All of us need such courage to face the journey and all that waits for us on the sea and beyond. But the key to life is to get in the boat."

Ramon paused and took a deep breath before continuing.

"I have been thinking about boats and courage and islands this weekend, wondering how it's going to end for my homeland, my island, and for us. We're all really in the same boat, you and I and the people of Cuba, unsure of how it's going to end, unsure of what happens next, unsure of what we will become, but grateful for the opportunity to explore what is, after all, a great beginning. A great commencement.

"What a gift it is to have the chance to begin, to take the first step on a great journey. I think we sometimes forget how fortunate we are in America to live our lives without a director looking over our shoulder, shaping our next move or anticipating it. There is no script. Most of us here in America are free to live unscripted lives, taking our boats where we want, avoiding the storms or meeting them head on. How's it going to end, we wonder. What will we become? And the truth is, we don't really want to know. We really wouldn't want it any other way.

"The poet Mary Oliver says it best in her poem, 'A Summer Day':

Who made the world?
Who made the swan, and the black bear?
Who made the grasshopper?
This grasshopper, I mean—
the one who has flung herself out of the grass,
the one who is eating sugar out of my hand,
who is moving her jaws back and forth instead of up
     and down—
who is gazing around with her enormous and
     complicated eyes.

Now she lifts her pale forearms and thoroughly washes
   her face.
Now she snaps her wings open, and floats away.
I don't know exactly what a prayer is.
I do know how to pay attention, how to fall down
into the grass, how to kneel in the grass,
how to be idle and blessed, how to stroll through the
   fields,
which is what I have been doing all day.
Tell me, what else should I have done?
Doesn't everything die at last, and too soon?
Tell me, what is it you plan to do
With your one wild and precious life?

Ramon stopped and paused. Then he read the last two
lines again.

"Tell me, what is it you plan to do with your one wild
and precious life? Let us honor our parents by living our lives
to the fullest, using our gifts in the service of others to make
the world a better place. That is the best way to thank our
parents for what we owe them. And let us hope the people
of Cuba will soon have the chance to enjoy a future uncon-
strained by a director or a script. May we all be blessed with
wild and precious lives. And may our paths on the journey
cross often."

Ramon bowed his head and said thank you. The crowd
erupted in applause. Ruth Lieber fought off the urge to rush
over to Ramon and embrace him. She let the president shake
his hand. She watched as Bob Bachman came up to shake his
hand. She watched as the crowd of students surged around
him. She watched as the cameras clicked and flashed. And she

watched as the older woman came down from the stands and made her way up to the stage. The woman was still wiping her eyes. She stood on the outside of the ring of students who were congratulating Ramon. What a journey her unscripted life had been. Ruth went over to her and gently touched her shoulder.

"Ms. Fernandez?"

The woman smiled and nodded. Ruth reached out and gently opened a path to Ramon so that Celia Fernandez could embrace her son.

13

HOW'S IT GOING TO END?

It was twenty years before Ramon Fernandez discovered what Ruth Lieber really had in mind all those times the two of them had talked economics that spring when Ramon was graduating and preparing for Wimbledon. Ramon was in the Bay Area on business. He flew into San Jose on a perfect August day, rented a car and, before heading into San Francisco, stopped off in Palo Alto for a taste of nostalgia. Even without Amy, it was sweet to visit the Baylands and feel the wind whipping across the Bay and the marsh, the swallows on the wing and the marsh alive with shorebirds. Then he headed to campus.

Parking on campus had only gotten harder, but he found a spot near enough to the tennis center and walked over. A group of kids, part of a summer camp, were playing on the side courts. Center court was empty. He was surprised at the surge of emotion that washed over him as he sat in the stands, losing himself in the memories. Then he stopped off to see Coach, who ribbed him about how he'd struggle today to go five sets with those five extra pounds around his middle.

Instead of heading back to the car, he found himself on the familiar path over to the provost's office. He knew Ruth had been retired for, what was it now, twenty years? For a while they had stayed in touch via e-mail. He had read the books she had loaned him and asked for more suggestions for understanding wealth and poverty. But the e-mails became less frequent as Ramon's life got busier.

There was nothing grand or palatial about the provost's office. It was in a low-lying unobtrusive building that could belong to any department on campus. Ramon went in.

"Can I help you?" the receptionist asked, looking up. Then she recognized him. "Ramon Fernandez! How are you?"

"I'm fine."

"You look like you could still go five sets." Ramon smiled at the power of perspective. "What can I do for you?"

"Just wanted to know if you ever hear from Ruth Lieber. Do you have any idea how she's doing?"

"I still get mail for her. Maybe once a month. I forward it along, but every once in a while, she stops in for it herself. She's getting up there. She had a hip replaced. Both of them, now that I think of it. But her mind is fine. As she likes to say, her better faculties are intact."

"So she still lives around here?"

"Oh, yes. But she's in Sea Ranch for August."

"Sea Ranch?"

"It's about three hours north of San Francisco on the coast. She spends every August up there with her family."

"The next time she stops by, would you tell her that Ramon Fernandez sends her regards?"

"Why don't you call her? She'd love to hear from you."

She wrote the number down for him. Well, why not call her, Ramon wondered as he walked to his car. But he didn't. He could only think of reasons not to call. Would she really want to hear from him? It would be wrong to call her when she was with her family. She must be well over eighty now, probably hard of hearing. Trying to talk on a cell would be awkward. His mind was soon thinking about his schedule for the rest of the day and he forgot about the piece of paper with Ruth Lieber's number he had stuffed in his wallet.

When his last meeting was over, Ramon parked in a garage off of Sutter and just roamed around the city for a while, hitting spots he remembered, tasting that bittersweet candy we call memory. Everything still the same but not the same at all. Without realizing it, he found himself heading toward the wharf area. Incredibly, Pedro's was still there, the place where he and Amy used to dance. Pedro was gone, but someone else had kept the same mix of grit and charm. Ramon sat at the bar and drank a cold beer and thought about Amy.

Too late to call her on the East Coast. But then he remembered Ruth Lieber. The beer emboldened him. He wandered outside. Sitting on a bench looking out over the water, he dialed the number.

"Hello."

"May I speak to Ruth Lieber?"

"Speaking."

"Ruth, it's Ramon Fernandez."

The silence on the other end of the line made Ramon wonder if he had made a mistake. He had played in the finals on center court at Wimbledon five times, but the silence gave him butterflies.

"Ramon." The way she said it warmed him. "Ramon," she said again. "What a treat. It is so good to hear from you. Where are you?"

"I'm actually sitting on a bench down by Fisherman's Wharf savoring the night air. Thinking about those talks we

used to have. Wondering how you've been. Feeling bad that
I haven't called or written or e-mailed or—"

"Forget about it. You want to make it up to me?"

"Sure, what's up?"

"Doing anything tomorrow?"

"Sitting on the red-eye pretending that I'm trying to sleep.
I don't know why I keep fooling myself into thinking it's a
good way to travel."

"Sorry. Just thought if you had some free time, I'd get a
ride into the city, get a cup of coffee."

Maybe it was the beer on an empty stomach or the wind
in his hair or Alcatraz showing through the haze on the water
or just those twenty-year-old memories. Whatever it was,
Ramon postponed his trip home for a day, spent the night
in Sausalito, and drove up to Sea Ranch the next morning,
snaking up those long switchbacks on the ridges up the coast
on Highway 1, the most beautiful road in the world, north or
south, but here, north, you could see cows wishing they had
shorter legs on one side so they could graze better on the 60
degree hillsides. He had never been on this stretch before. It
was less grand than the road to Big Sur, but more intimate.

He found the house and walked around back, where he
found Ruth Lieber sitting in a weathered Adirondack chair,
on a deck looking out over the Pacific. Ramon was shocked
to see how small she was. She had never been a large woman,
but age had made her even smaller. She looked up. She
couldn't leap to her feet. Those artificial hips and the rest of
her weren't up to it. But Ramon was thrilled to see the same
fire in those eyes he had seen before. Her smile told him just
how glad she was that he had made the trip.

"Tell me everything," she said, pointing to the chair next to her.

So he did. She knew of his four wins at Wimbledon and the two U.S Opens. She wanted to know about everything else. He and Amy had married while she was still in medical school. After he had quit the tour and started the tennis academy in Miami, they had two children, a boy and a girl. He told her about the academy's success and how much time they were spending in Havana. Ramon would give tennis demonstrations on the weekend. During the week, he worked with local officials on expanding sports opportunities for kids. Amy volunteered at clinics working with the poor, giving vaccinations, setting a broken finger, finding kids a place to get a good meal, anything that was needed.

Amy loved Cuba. Thought it was almost as beautiful as California. She wasn't thrilled with the humidity and she hated the lizards. But she loved the land and the people. She always encouraged any opportunities or trips that would take him there. They were very happy. He was very blessed. Yes, his mother was still alive. She had moved back to Havana in a house Ramon had bought for her. Amy and Ramon spent so much time in Cuba, that they had bought a house on the same street as his mom.

Then Ruth talked about her retirement, her family, her occasional op-ed or letter to the editor and how she still checked in with the university from time to time to let them know she was still up and about. A silence. As if on cue, the sun burned a hole through the fog and suddenly the Pacific came to life, a deep aquamarine against the lighter sky.

"So is the rumor true?" Ruth asked finally, breaking the silence.

"Rumor? What rumor?"

"The rumor that you're thinking of challenging President Gonzalez, a year from this February."

"Now where would you read something like that, Ruth? You're spending too much time on the Internet."

"No doubt. But you didn't answer my question. Is the rumor true?"

He smiled. His meetings in San Francisco had gone well. He had received enough pledges of support that he thought he could actually make a go of it. An election in any democracy, young or old, was inevitably unpredictable. But he was ready for the risks. He hesitated to tell her—he had the impression she wasn't a big fan of politicians. Ramon looked around, pretending to be worried they might be overheard.

"Can you keep a secret?" he asked, finally.

"Who am I going to tell?" she asked, gesturing toward the ocean and meadows. "The seals sunning on the rocks? The deer browsing in the meadow?" For a moment, her eyes narrowed and the smile fell away but Ramon was looking out at the sparkling water and missed it. She fought off the urge to press him. She waited.

"I'm going to do it. Amy knows, but I haven't even told my mother. She—"

Ramon stopped in mid-sentence. There was a look on Ruth's face he had never seen before. A look of delight. A look of triumph. He had seen that look on center court on the face of his opponents the few times he had fallen short in a Grand Slam event. He had seen it on his own face in the paper or on ESPN when he had won. It was a look of deep satisfaction, a look of power, of mastery shining through a veneer of nonchalance as if mastery and triumph are nothing unusual. Suddenly, he felt the hair on his arms stand up. Then the back of his neck.

"Are you all right, Ramon? I won't tell anyone. I promise," she said.

He muttered something under his breath in Spanish.

"You knew," he said. "You knew," he repeated, shaking his head in wonder. "But how could you know?" he said as much to himself as to her.

"Oh, it was just a rumor on some blog I was reading, I was—"

"No. You knew back then. Twenty years ago. You knew. How did you know?" He smiled and then started laughing. "How could you possibly know?"

Ruth looked away. She watched the sun duck back behind its foggy veil. Then she turned and looked at Ramon Fernandez.

"Ever take an American history course?"

"Sure, in high school." What did that have to do with their conversations of twenty years ago? She wasn't going to get away with it this time. "How did you know?"

"It's a funny thing," Ruth continued, ignoring his question. The first president of the United States? George Washington. The most famous American of his day. The second president? John Adams. The third president? Thomas Jefferson. Then James Madison. Then James Monroe. Then John Quincy Adams." What was her point? "Do you know how far into American history you have to go to find a president who wasn't a Founder, a relative of a Founder, or a war hero?"

"I have no idea," Ramon admitted, amused by the digression.

"I have no idea, either. Haven't checked in years, but if memory serves, it was Martin Van Buren and the election of 1836. Some of those early presidents were giants. The cream of the cream. But some were merely famous. I don't think for a minute that they were the best available men for the job. But they had name recognition. Most of them had accomplished something. That helped. But you don't need to be much of a political scientist to understand something profound about the electorate, especially in the early days of a country's history. The electorate is very risk averse. Voters don't have the time or the incentive to research the candidates the way we might think they should. They like someone they've heard of, someone they can trust."

"Meaning?"

"Even when Castro was alive, you were the best-known Cuban on the planet." Ruth let that sink in before continuing.

"I didn't know you'd ever run for president of Cuba. But there were some things back then I did know. I knew Castro wouldn't live forever. I didn't know if a democracy of any respectability would eventually fall into place on Cuba or if it would survive. But I figured there was a chance. And I knew you would have more than name recognition. Name recognition was what made it easy for Gonzalez. But you also have brains. You have charisma. I saw what you did to that crowd back in front of the Big Box building on campus that time. Plus, you care. You care about your country. I saw that on that Sunday back in June at graduation, years ago. So did I know? Of course not. But I thought there was a pretty good chance you could be at least a U.S. senator from California or Florida if you wanted."

Ramon leaned back in his chair, amazed that for all of his respect for Ruth Lieber's skills, he had still managed to underestimate her one more time.

"Let me tell you something," she continued. "A confession of sorts. Knowing how the world works isn't all that valuable. Understanding how prices emerge, understanding how innovation works, isn't all that useful. I remember one editor who rejected a manuscript of mine, early on in my career. I wrote a little primer on economics for the general public based on my principles class. She said it was a lovely book, but it wouldn't help people lose weight, reduce their golf score, improve their love life, or make them rich. It wouldn't sell. The people who understand what we talked about twenty years ago, a few economists and a few students who fall in love with the paradoxes and surprises of serious economics, we just enjoy that knowledge for its own sake. Like being able to tell an osprey from a seagull or being able to name the constellations at night. It's part of being a civilized human being. But understanding economics does have one small area of real practical application. It helps you vote wisely. Having some idea of the complexity of the world teaches you to be skeptical of the quick fix and to understand that most political promises come with more strings than a yo-yo factory. That's very useful knowledge to have in the voting booth. But there is one place it's even more useful. And that is in the Oval Office or whatever shape it is in Cuba. I wanted—"

Her voice broke. She slowly raised herself up out of her chair using all of her strength and stood before him, her eyes now level with his. The tears streamed down her face, but she spoke through them. "I spent the early part of my career writing scholarly papers for scholarly journals that a handful of scholars found interesting. But in the classroom, I taught thousands of students over the years about the complexity of the world. Some of them took my classes to fulfill some requirement for a degree. Some wanted to take an economics class because they thought it would look good on a resume. But some took my classes because they wanted to understand. I could tell that you wanted to understand. And I figured someday, someday that understanding would serve you in good stead. I wanted you to have the tools I thought you'd need some day. I couldn't give that to you in a handful of conversations. But I thought maybe I would spark something that would catch flame later. That's all a teacher can ever hope for. And in my wildest dreams, I imagined living long enough to be able to see what would happen to you. And now I've been blessed to reach that day."

Ruth wiped away the tears and sat back down. Ramon reached across the gap between their two chairs and took her hand. He said nothing. He couldn't decide whether her effort twenty years ago was the most touching or the most quixotic or foolish or brilliant thing he had ever heard of. He looked at the woman sitting next to him and marveled that she had spent some of her time on a kid way back when. Then he told her how much it amazed him. Told her what he was thinking back then, of how the protest and Heavy Weather and his speech seemed like the most important thing in all the world until Castro died and how he grew up a little after that. How when you're twenty-two you think, no, *you know* you're the center of the universe. Until you get a little older and you find out it's not quite true. Is there any lesson more important to fully understand, if you want to be a grown-up?

Then they talked in earnest about all the challenges facing Ramon in the election and what might follow. Finally, Ramon had to go. He had a plane to catch. He hugged her and said good-bye, knowing he would probably never see her again, but promising to write and call and yes, ask her advice if all went well and he actually won.

Long after Ramon had left, Ruth sat watching the water, watching the ocean swallow the sun, until the air became cooler, the wind rose, and the stars came out. How strange life is, she thought. You study hard in school and get good grades. You go to graduate school with dreams of doing great work. You do great work, or at least decent work, writing those research papers that you know when you write them will change the world, and then you discover the truth that the world is very hard to change. Only a handful of scholars have that gift. The rest are adding a crumb here or there to the pile that others add to in the same way. Oh, there's prestige and a little bit of glory and not a small amount of money along the way for the best. But only the work of the best of the best really amounts to anything.

And all those hours in the classroom, all those glory-free hours lecturing and hectoring and prodding and urging the students to see the world through the lens that you find so marvelous! Tedious hours of grading, tedious hours of office hours where too many students arrive merely to avoid a bad grade. So many of those hours come to nothing, like a storm that scatters the seeds of a tree. So many fall on rocky ground or on unproductive soil or get washed away by the inevitable rain that is too heavy or not heavy enough. And some seeds can fall in the perfect place for taking root, but it takes fire to set them free. And the fire never comes.

A teacher has to take solace in knowing that some of those seeds, incredibly, take root. Some insights get washed away in the storm of life's distractions. But every once in a while, with a good enough teacher, you get a redwood or a sequoia of a student where your ideas take hold and make a difference. And if you are really lucky, you get to see the tree grow to maturity.

Ruth had no illusions about living much longer and seeing the rest of the story. But she had seen plenty already. She had been blessed to live long enough to see her hand in shaping a life that was wilder and more precious than even she could have imagined when she first crossed paths with Ramon Fernandez.

In the Talmud it says that it is better to be a perfume-maker than a tanner of leather. Better to have a sweet-smelling job even if, as Adam Smith pointed out a thousand or so years later, the tanner's pay is higher than it otherwise would be to get people to pass up a sweeter-smelling way to spend one's time. Ruth Lieber gloried in knowing she had spent her life in a sweet-smelling job, working with the perfume of knowledge and wisdom. The rewards were more than enough.

A few miles down the coast, Ramon pushed his rental car through the turns of Highway 1. He was going as fast as he could go, not because he was in a hurry—he had plenty of time to make his flight—but for the pleasure he got from controlling the car, a skill he had always had. The road was so steep and the turns so sharp, Ramon almost felt he was skiing—slaloming down the coast, the water on his right all the time and not much traffic on the road. A mix of danger and delight—and if he was honest with himself, delightful precisely because of the danger.

Then he slowed suddenly. What was he doing? Talking with Ruth had thrown him back in time. But he wasn't so young anymore. He had a wife and kids to get home to, and a country waiting, perhaps, to embrace him. He slowed. Take your time, he thought, focus on the road.

His mind wandered anyway. He thought of the great ocean on his right. And to the left, the great trees towering over him. Keep going, he thought, and saw Yosemite, the way he and Amy had seen it for the first time, junior year, Half Dome at sunset from Glacier Point, a sentinel over that valley. Then up and over the Rockies, skimming over the prairies of the Midwest in his mind's eye, heading southeast, now he could see Miami, the neighborhood where he and his mother had spent all those days and nights and somehow managed to keep going, almost there, ah there it is, that small strait of water, the island waiting, a jewel in the coral water.

The image of his parents came to him, the picture he had of the two of them, young, deeply in love, walking along the Malecon when everything still seemed possible. When Ramon was younger, he would ask his mother for stories about his father, his baseball career, how they had met. He loved the baseball stories, but the story of how they had met always stuck with him and he had heard it so many times, he could play it back in his head whenever he wanted.

"I was invited to a party," his mother would begin. "It was in this gorgeous old mansion right on the beach. It was 1960. I was eighteen years old. The revolution was barely a year old and there was still more excitement than despair—hope was still triumphing over experience."

"You were only eighteen?"

"I had no idea of what I was going to do with my life. But when I saw your father at that party, I knew one thing. I was going to marry him. Or at least I'd try."

"So he was at the party?"

"Anyone who was anyone was at that party. But your father wasn't just anyone. Only Castro got more attention that night from the other guests. And maybe not even Castro. Everyone wanted a piece of Jose Fernandez. He was twenty-four. Not quite in the prime of his career, but already a star among stars. And you can't imagine how much Cubans love baseball."

"Go on."

"The party spilled out of the house onto the patio overlooking the ocean. Starry night, orchestra playing."

"What was the orchestra playing?" Ramon knows the answer, but he asks anyway.

"It was 'Begin the Beguine.' It wasn't long before you couldn't play a song written by an American. Had to be Cuban, and only certain Cubans. But these were early days and Cole Porter was still OK. Something about that song got into my bones. I had to dance. And I'd had a drink or two. I wasn't used to drinking, but my father was talking to a group of businessmen. And I was watching Jose Fernandez. He was surrounded by a bunch of men. I could tell they were talking about baseball."

"How could you tell?"

"Your father was in his batting stance, an imaginary bat cocked, and ready to unleash that magnificent swing. Then he was the pitcher hopelessly hoping to steer a fastball past a stick of lightning. He was recounting some big at-bat. I edged closer to the circle of listening men as they devoured his words, basking in his presence. The drinks, the music, the stars—they all conspired to make me braver. Even braver than I usually was."

"What did you do?" Ramon asked, keeping to the formula.

"I asked him to dance."

"And he said yes?"

"No, he just smiled and kept talking. But I stood my ground. I wanted to slip out of the circle and run home. But I stood my ground. And the orchestra started up with a new song that stopped his story in mid-sentence and made him turn to me."

"What song? Do you remember?"

"I do. It was 'Beyond the Sea.' I loved that song. Still do. Your father must have liked it, too. He stopped his story and turned to me and asked me for my name. Celia, I answered. You want to dance, Celia, he asked."

"And you said yes?"

"I said nothing. My heart was pounding. Instead of answering, I gave him my hand and followed him out onto the dance floor. I gave him my hand and my heart followed."

His mother always ended the story on the dance floor. But Ramon always imagined the two young people after the dance had ended, holding hands, looking out at the ocean, that ocean that held the promise that all shorelines hold, the promise of tomorrow, the boundless horizon, the crash of the ever-changing unpredictable waves. There was no way they could imagine what really lay beyond the sea, what lay just beyond tomorrow. Love and marriage and birth. A death too soon, followed by drama and drudgery and then all the promise of America that his mother had given him. So much courage along the way in the face of that unknowable future. And now he was returning across that same sea to find out what would happen next. He thought of Amy and the children and all that was yet to come. I'm coming home, he murmured. I'm coming home.

Sources and Further Reading

This book is my attempt to give the beginner and the expert a better understanding of the role prices play in our lives—how they create harmony between the competing desires of consumers and entrepreneurs, and how they steer resources and knowledge to transform and sustain our standard of living. To learn more, start with Hayek's "The Use of Knowledge in Society" (from the *American Economic Review*, 1945) and Leonard Read's charming "I, Pencil," both available at Econlib.org. My analytical treatment of these ideas, at times combining Hayek's insights with traditional supply and demand analysis, is available at http://www.invisibleheart.com. Look for "Supply and Demand," "The Theory of the Firm," and "Prices and Knowledge." For a deep look at the role of knowledge in economic life, see *Knowledge and Decisions* (Basic Books, 1996) by Thomas Sowell. See also *The Wisdom of Crowds* (Doubleday, 2004) by James Surowiecki.

At the heart of this book is the concept of emergent order. If you'd like to learn more about emergent order, start with Hayek's *The Fatal Conceit: Errors of Socialism* (University of Chicago Press, 1989). Ignore the title—it's not really about socialism. For more popular treatments that touch on the general idea of emergence, read *Out of Control* (Perseus Books Group, 1995) by Kevin Kelly and *Emergence* (Scribner's, 2001) by Steven Johnson. The idea of emergence clearly affected Jane Jacobs's classic, *The Death and Life of Great American Cities* (Random House, 1961). Her later book, *The Nature of Economies* (Modern Library, 2000), explicitly explores emergence and the connection between nature and economics. Michael Rothschild's *Bionomics: Economy as Ecosystem* (Henry Holt, 1992) takes a similar approach. Both emphasize the organic, emergent, undesigned aspect of economics I try to capture here.

On economic growth, read Brad DeLong's unpublished essay, "Cornucopia: Increasing Wealth in the Twentieth Century," http://econ161.berkeley.edu/TCEH/2000/TCEH_2.html. It's full of fascinating data and insights into the transformation of our standard of living. Then read Paul Romer's "Economic Growth" from *The Concise Encyclopedia of Economics* (Liberty Fund, 2008) edited by David Henderson, and available on the web at EconLib.org. In that essay, Romer notes, "In 1985, I paid a thousand dollars per million transistors for memory in my computer. In 2005, I paid less than ten dollars per million." That hundred-fold drop is another example of the transformation of our standard of living via innovation. It's even more important than the fall in the real price of eggs. Paul and I discuss those ideas further in a podcast at EconTalk.org.

The essay by Robert Lucas, "Industrial Revolution: Past and Future," published by the Minneapolis Federal Reserve as part of their 2003 Annual Report, is an excellent introduction to the history of economic growth and how we got here from there. My podcast with Lucas on growth can be heard at EconTalk.org. Read *Pursuing Happiness* (Princeton University Press, 1993) by the underappreciated Stanley Lebergott. It's full of incredible facts, and his writing always delights. The whole book is fascinating, but I particularly recommend the first fifty-four pages of *The Bourgeois Virtues* (University of Chicago Press, 2006) by Deirdre McCloskey, a marvelous brief for how capitalism enriches our lives in material and spiritual ways. My final suggestion is Part II of Schumpeter's *Capitalism, Socialism, and Democracy* (Harper Perennial, 1962), some of the best one hundred pages ever written on the dynamics of capitalism.

This book was written before the financial crisis of 2008. For some observers, the crisis proves that capitalism has failed, and the idea of leaving many things alone has been irrevocably discredited. While many economists (including this one) overestimated the stability of the financial system, it was not unregulated or left alone.

The housing market, the underlying source of the crisis, was not left alone. The interested reader can find my essays on these topics and the implications for public policy at InvisibleHeart.com.

1 Thinking Outside the Box

I chose Home Depot as the first store that Ramon and Amy visit because Home Depot has stated that they do not raise prices and take advantage of customers after a hurricane or natural disaster. Large companies such as Home Depot and Wal-Mart often leave prices at their normal levels in the aftermath of a natural disaster to enhance their reputation, at least among customers who get to the store early. But in recent years, prices have probably risen less after natural disasters because of competition and technology—better inventory control and weather prediction have lowered the costs of getting supplies quickly to affected areas. I thank Spencer England for pointing this out to me.

After Hurricane Isabel hit Washington, D.C. in September 2003, one of my students whose husband was a contractor told me how disgusted her husband had been with the high prices people were charging for generators. Surely a contractor would want a backup energy supply, I said. Surely he had paid the high price. No, she explained, he already had a backup and had been considering buying a second backup. But at double the regular price, he passed. Someone else got that generator and I got a richer understanding of higher prices.

2 Out of Control

The story of the graduate student in Ruth's library is adapted from a similar story people tell at the University of Rochester about Stan Engerman.

Ruth's story of the pencil is my homage to the classic "I, Pencil" by Leonard Read, mentioned above. Read's first-person story of how a pencil requires the cooperation of millions is probably the most charming story of how the production of a simple product requires the complex coordination of thousands of individuals working together without knowing each other or sharing the same goals. I trace a number of similar examples going back to Adam Smith and the woolen coat in the essay "A Marvel of Cooperation: How Order Emerges Without a Conscious Planner" at the Library of Economics and Liberty (Econlib.org).

The details about the assembly of the Dixon Ticonderoga pencil come from a tour of the Dixon Ticonderoga plant in Versailles, Missouri. I want to thank Rick Joyce of Dixon Ticonderoga for arranging the tour and Frank Murphy, the plant manager, for his time and patience in explaining the workings of the plant. One of the most striking aspects of the tour, which mirrors other tours I've had of an automobile factory and a bottling plant, is how few people work in a modern factory. Everything is mechanized and computerized. The main task of the handful of workers on the job is to monitor the process. When Leonard Read wrote his story, a cedar slat had eight grooves and the slat sandwich produced eight pencils. Frank Murphy told me that it once was only seven. Today, because of the improved precision of the saws that cut the slats, the same slat produces ten pencils, another example of innovation lowering costs.

3   Birds of a Feather

I have spent many pleasant hours at the Baylands where Ramon and Amy meet and talk. It was there that a birder told me that he had seen the stilts and godwits and avocets create a makeshift flock on the fly to chase away a hawk. I forgot to get his name and I hope he was telling the truth. If you are an authority on birds or an avid birder and can confirm this behavior, please drop me a note.

4   Inconceivable

For more on ants and the division of labor, listen to my podcast with Deborah Gordon at EconTalk.org.

This chapter draws heavily on Hayek's "The Use of Knowledge in Society," which explains how prices coordinate dispersed knowledge.

The housing market doesn't literally clear at every point in time as the discussion of housing prices might suggest. I use housing as the example because, despite the incredible diversity of the housing stock in all American cities, competition plays a central role in what a house sells for, not the kindness or greed of the buyer or seller.

Ruth Lieber's discussion of housing focuses on this competition between buyers and sellers and the resulting orderly pattern of prices in a particular housing market. Her discussion leaves out the role public policy plays in distorting the price of housing. A partial catalog of these policies in the United States can be found under the category "Government intervention in housing" at my blog, CafeHayek.com.

The birthing story is based on a true story. The names have been changed to protect the innocent and the guilty.

The story of the woman who died waiting for flu vaccine and mention of the other hospitalizations is at http://www.usatoday.com/news/health/2004-10-16-flu-wait-death_x.htm.

7   The Goose That Lays the Golden Eggs

There are no precise estimates of the change in the standard of living of the average American over the last century. Per-capita GDP has increased roughly sevenfold since 1900 (Louis D. Johnston and Samuel H. Williamson, "The Annual Real and Nominal GDP for the United States, 1790–Present," Economic History Services, October 2005; URL: http://www.eh.net/hmit/gdp/). Brad DeLong, in his "Cornucopia" essay mentioned above, reports a slightly greater than four-fold increase in output per worker that he boosts to a seven- to eightfold increase in standard of living when the shorter workweek of today is taken into account.

These estimates, of course, are only averages when we would prefer a median measure of standard of living that does not over-weight the upper end of the income distribution. Either way, they are flawed because of the fundamental challenge of controlling for quality changes discussed by Ruth and Ramon. The average or median income person today can buy a lot more stuff than the average or median income person in 1900. But the quality differences that make measuring that change a challenge are so qualitatively different that treating them quantitatively is almost impossible, as Ruth's example of the iPod versus the strolling musicians illustrates. DeLong puts it this way—take a person with median income today and give that person the median income of 1900. They're worse off. What multiple of 1900's median income would they need to make them equally well-off as they are today? It's not clear that that number even exists. Would that person accept ten times the median income of 1900? Would an average American today give up the iPod and antibiotics and air travel and satellite TV and modern childbirth and dentistry and heart surgery in exchange even for the opportunity to be the richest person of 1900?

So the qualitative summary of changes in access to refrigeration and medical care and central heating and so on may be more informative for giving us a feel of the change in human material well-being over the last century. Those comparisons come primarily from work by Stanley Lebergott. The figure on flush toilets is from Lebergott's *Pursuing Happiness* (PH), table II.15. Housework figures are from PH, table 8.1. The workweek of housewives is from PH, page 58. The figure on running water and gallons hauled is from PH, page 100. Figures on ice boxes is from PH, page 113. Farm and nonfarm workweek is from Lebergott's *The American Economy* (Princeton University Press, 1976), page 90. Data on households taking in a lodger are from *The American Economy*, page 93.

The data on maternal mortality and infant mortality are taken from "Achievements in Public Health, 1900–1999: Healthier Mothers and Babies" from the Morbidity and Mortality Weekly Report from the CDC (October 1, 1999): http://www.cdc.gov/mmwR/preview/mmwrhtml/mm4838a2.htm.

The idea that the palpable differences between rich and poor are relatively small—the story of the waiter and the donor—comes from an insight of Don Boudreaux's. The number of books published in 1900 is taken from The Annual American Catalog, 1900–1909, accessed on Google Books. The current figure is from Bowker.com.

The figures on the poor's access to washers, dryers, dishwashers, air conditioning, and so on are taken from table 2-4 (p. 66) and table 3-12 (p. 162) of the American Housing Survey of the United States: 2005, available at http://www.census.gov/prod/2006pubs/h150-05.pdf. Access to air conditioning for all Americans in 1970 is taken from table A-1 of the Annual Housing Survey: 1973 available at http://www.census.gov/prod/www/abs/h150.html.

The data on teacher's salaries in 1900 ($328 a year) are taken from *Historical Statistics of the United States, Millennial Edition*, table Ba4320-4334. At forty-two weeks per year, that's $1.50 a day or roughly an hour to earn a dozen eggs at 21 cents per dozen, the 1900 price. The egg price is from *Historical Statistics of the United States, Colonial Times to 1970* (U.S. Department of Commerce, Bicentennial Edition, 1975) in Series E 187-202, page 213. So it took a school teacher in 1900 about one-sixth of a day, or a little more than an hour, to earn a dozen eggs. According to surveys by the National Education Association, the average school teacher in 2005 made about $48,000 a year. That's $20–30 an hour (depending on hours worked), or 2–3 minutes to earn a dozen eggs at $1 per dozen, the figure used in the text.

According to the *Historical Statistics of the United States, Millennial*

Edition (table Ba4335–4360, Cambridge University Press, 2006), the average domestic servant made about $240 per year. At seventy-two hours per week, fifty-one weeks per year, that comes to a little under seven cents an hour, or three hours to buy a dozen eggs.

Data and background on egg production come from Michael Rothschild's *Bionomics*, and conversations with Chad Gregory, senior vice president of United Egg Producers, Bob Gornichec of Buckeye Egg Farms, and Linus Hart, whose experience in the egg industry goes back to 1949. Today's largest farms have over 5 million hens. The largest hen houses have between 700,000 and 800,000 birds under a single roof. According to Chad Gregory, 3–5 workers oversee up to 1.5 million chickens in the egg-laying part of a modern egg operation. I've rounded that to two workers overseeing 800,000 hens. As in the pencil factory, those two workers do little more than keep an eye on the computerized system that feeds the hens, medicates the hens, collects the waste for sale as fertilizer, collects the eggs, and transports the eggs via conveyor belt to the part of the farm where the eggs are cleaned, graded, and put into cartons. It was Linus Hart who asked me the rhetorical question, "You know what the problem with our industry is?" and answered it, saying, "Too many eggs." Ah, competition. The boon of consumers and bane of suppliers.

I use the figure of eighty eggs per hen per year for America in 1900 and the Third World today. According to USDA figures reported in *American Poultry History, 1823–1973* (American Poultry Historical Society, 1974, page 213), the average productivity of American hens per year in 1910 was about eighty-three eggs. I have also seen estimates of fifty eggs per year per hen in poor countries at various points in the twentieth century.

I made up the David Kornfeld and Tom Warson stories, though both draw on experiences I had working with entrepreneurs at Washington University's Olin School of Business. I got the idea for the essence of the Kornfeld story from a story in *My Grandfather's Blessings* (Riverhead Trade, 2001) by Rachel Naomi Remen.

10   No Host No Problem

To read more about development and poverty, read William Easterly's *The Elusive Quest for Growth* (MIT Press, 2001) and Hernando de Soto's *The Mystery of Capital* (Basic Books, 2000).

Ruth Lieber emphasizes the host-less part of the innovation story that has transformed the standard of living in America in the twentieth century, though she admits that publicly funded research also played a role. Some argue that such research is a crucial factor in the transformation of our standard of living. A study that tries to measure the importance of public versus private research would be very helpful.

At the end of this chapter, Ruth and Ramon get on the computer and look at studies on inequality, mobility, and changes in America's standard of living in recent years. My empirical summary of these issues, "Half-Full: An Illustrated Guide to Inequality, Mobility, and America's Standard of Living," can be found at invisibleheart.com.

A THOUGHT ON GOD, EVOLUTION, AND EMERGENT ORDER

A lot of the people I know who are interested in emergent order are either ardent atheists or deeply religious. I understand why atheists are comforted by the possibility of order emerging without design. But emergent order is consistent with religious beliefs as well. Just because order can emerge without design does not mean that all order must be undesigned. Nor does emergent order rule out a role for God in designing the backdrop for what emerges. You can either admire the wonder of evolution and the wonder of the price system as proof that the world works fine without anyone being in charge in the fullest sense of that phrase, or you can be grateful to God for embedding such wonders in our world.

Acknowledgments

I am grateful to the Olin Foundation and the Weidenbaum Center at Washington University in St. Louis, where this book was born.

This book came to maturity at George Mason University. The economics department at George Mason is an incredible place to work. Much of my understanding of Hayek and emergence has emerged from conversations with Don Boudreaux, who has a deep grasp of the topic and a passion for talking about it. I am grateful for those conversations and for Don's role in creating an amazingly open-minded place to work that honors good economics in all its forms.

I want to thank Menlo Smith for his support, his inspiration, and his expectations.

I want to thank Deirdre McCloskey for my first real taste of price theory as an engine of analysis and for unknowingly helping me name one of the characters in this book.

I am grateful to the Mercatus Center at George Mason University for support and for the opportunity to be part of Capital Hill Campus. My lectures there helped me understand many of the ideas in this book and improved the exposition here.

I want to thank Emilio Pacheco and Liberty Fund for the opportunity to be part of the Library of Economics and Liberty (econlib. org)—many of my essays there helped me with ideas in this book. I also want to thank Dwight Lee and Andy Rutten, who organized the incredibly stimulating Liberty Fund conference in May 2000, "The Communication of Economics," that got me interested in the mystery of how knowledge gets used by markets.

Much of this story is set on the campus of Stanford University. It's a somewhat mythical Stanford of the future—undergraduates do not speak at commencement these days. There is no Big Box Executive Center at Stanford. I am grateful to the Hoover Institution and its Director, John Raisian, for support in writing this book. The opportunity to spend summers at Hoover has enhanced this book as well.

I want to thank Dick Gould, director of tennis at Stanford University, for helpful insights into high-level college tennis. Any tennis errors are my own.

I want to thank Bruce Yandle for Ruth's line about loving her job but if she weren't paid, she'd stop showing up. I heard the line about honoring your parents by what you become from Rollie Massimino at a soccer practice forty years ago. The idea for cool bicycle helmets for kids came from Chris O' Leary.

I began this book as a dialogue between a teacher and a student sitting on a bench talking about economics. Gary Belsky complained that all they did was sit on the bench. So I took Ruth and Ramon off the bench. Steve Saletta complained that all they did was talk. So I followed them around when they left the bench and saw what else they did. I'm grateful to Gary and Steve for those spurs to improve the book.

Numerous readers gave me feedback and encouragement along the way. I want to thank Susan Anderson, Eliana Balla, Lee Benham, Don Boudreaux, Penny Britell, Emily Brooks, Bryan Caplan, Art Carden, Tyler Cowen, Lauren Chrissos, Zev Fredman, Milton Friedman, Phyllis Terry Friedman, Lora Ivanova, Jonathan Katz, Noel Kolak, Moshe Looks, Richard Mahoney, Deirdre McCloskey, Kelly Mesa, Christine Moseley, John Nye, Emily Pitlick, Kathy Ratte, Gina Yannitell Reinhardt, Morgan Rose, Andy Rutten, Steve Saletta, Bevis Schock, Tara Sinclair, Triya Venkatraman, Jeff Weiss, and Ann West.

I am grateful to Seth Ditchik of Princeton University Press for his encouragement, patience, and tenacity, especially when it came to the title.

I'm grateful to Gary Belsky, Joe Roberts, Shirley Roberts, and Ted Roberts for multiple readings of the manuscript and extremely insightful detailed comments and insights.

I'm especially grateful to Sharon and the kids for numerous comments on numerous drafts, for bearing the costs of all the time I spent on the saga of Ruth and Ramon, and for patiently helping me reject dozens of titles that weren't quite as good as *The Price of Everything*. Sharon, this book would mean nothing without you. Kids, I hope that when you come of age, America is still a place where dreams can still come true because there is no weaver of dreams.

About the Author

Russell Roberts (roberts@gmu.edu) is Professor of Economics at George Mason University, J. Fish and Lillian F. Smith Distinguished Scholar at George Mason's Mercatus Center, and a research fellow at Stanford University's Hoover Institution.

In addition to *The Price of Everything*, he is the author of *The Invisible Heart: An Economic Romance* (MIT Press, 2001) and *The Choice: A Fable of Free Trade and Protectionism* (3rd ed., Prentice Hall, 2006).

Roberts blogs at Cafe Hayek (http://www.cafehayek.com). His weekly podcasts are at EconTalk.org. He is the features editor and a founding advisory board member of the Library of Economics and Liberty (http://www.econlib.org). He archives his writing at InvisibleHeart.com.